£16.95

map wise

ACCELERATED LEARNING THROUGH VISIBLE THINKING

OLIVER CAVIGLIOLI
& IAN HARRIS

This book is based on the MapWise course that is run by Model Learning, the authors' company. The exercises presented in this book are the intellectual property of Model Learning. If you are interested in running a course, or in purchasing a copyright licence and photocopy masters of the exercises for your school, please contact Model Learning directly:

Model Learning
P O Box 5346
Brentwood
Essex
CM14 5RW
Tel/fax: 01277 202812
email: info@modellearning.com

Published by Network Educational Press Ltd
P O Box 635
Stafford
ST16 1BF

First published 2000
Reprinted 2001

Every effort has been made to contact copyright holders of materials reproduced in this book. The publishers apologise for any omissions and will be pleased to rectify them at the earliest opportunity. Please see page 209 for a comprehensive list of references and acknowledgements.

Editor: Gina Walker
Design: Neil Hawkins, Network Educational Press
Illustrations: Oliver Caviglioli

Printed in Great Britain by
MPG Books Ltd., Bodmin, Cornwall.

"Map me no maps, Sir,
my head is a map,
a map of the whole world."

Henry Fielding
Rape upon Rape (1730)

Acknowledgements

Together

We would like to acknowledge the contribution made to personal learning by the men and women around the world who lead the Landmark Forum – the most profoundly educational course we have experienced.

We would like to acknowledge Tony Buzan for his life-long commitment to, and promotion of, cognitive cartography.

We are deeply grateful for, and highly appreciative of, the editorial skills of Gina Walker.

Oliver

I would like to thank my Father, François, for thrilling me with the magic of his marks on paper and inspiring me with his unlimited creativity.

I am grateful for the moment more than 20 years ago at the London Buddhist Centre when I saw, over Dharmarati's shoulder, the possibilities of graphically beautiful maps.

This is for my family – Lyn, Pascal, Francesca and Roma – who are at the centre of my map.

Ian

This is for my Mum and Dad for being exactly who they are.

I would like to thank and acknowledge two teachers. For four years I team-taught 14–16 year olds with moderate learning difficulties and associated emotional and behavioural needs with Ros Ward. She opened my eyes to what is possible for teachers and learners, at a time when I didn't realise my eyes were shut. I worked with Barbara Hutson for two years and this book has come about indirectly but mainly because she realised, way before I did, the contribution that I could make to learning.

I am grateful to my friends for the interest and support they have all shown in their many different ways.

Contents

Foreword

The *Accelerated Learning Series* attempts to pull together new and innovative thinking about learning. The titles in the series offer contemporary solutions to old problems. The series is held together by the accelerated learning model which, in turn, is underwritten by an informed theoretical understanding.

The term 'accelerated learning' can be misleading. The method is not for a specific group of learners, nor for a given age range, nor for a category of perceived ability. The method is not about doing the same things faster. It is not about fast-tracking or about hot-housing. It is a considered, generic approach to learning based on research drawn from disparate disciplines and tested with different age groups and different ability levels in very different circumstances. As such, it can be adapted and applied to very different challenges.

The books in the *Accelerated Learning Series* build from the accelerated learning cycle. The cycle starts by attending to the physical, environmental and social factors in learning. It proposes the worth of a positive and supportive learning environment. It then deliberately attempts to connect to, and build upon, prior knowledge and understanding whilst presenting an overview of the learning challenge to come. Participants set positive outcomes and define targets towards reaching those outcomes. Information is then presented in visual, auditory and kinaesthetic modes and is reinforced through different forms of intelligent response. Frequent, structured opportunities to demonstrate understanding and to rehearse for recall are the concluding feature of the cycle.

Roger Sperry won the Nobel Prize in Medicine in 1981 for his research on the lateralisation of the human brain. In his acceptance speech, he noted that split-brain studies had brought new respect among educators for non-verbal aspects of the intellect. He said, "The more we learn, the more we recognise the unique complexity of any one individual intellect". He went on to add, "The individuality inherent in our brain networks makes that of fingerprints or facial features gross and simple by comparison. The need for education to identify, accommodate, and serve the differentially specialised forms of individual intellectual potential becomes increasingly evident." I believe *MapWise* sits within, and adds to, the accelerated learning philosophy of serving what Sperry described as the 'differentially specialised forms of individual intellectual potential'.

Accelerated learning makes the lofty claim to derive its structure from emerging brain research. In the books in the series you will see frequent reference to published work on the human brain. Terms like 'brain-based' are frequently used. This is at once a strength and a weakness. Scientific knowledge is not yet dealing in absolutes when it comes to findings about the human brain. Educators want solutions to their questions now. Science says 'maybe' or 'perhaps' or 'here is a model' or 'this is as much as we can say'. Occasionally however, findings are published which affirm an aspect of the thinking behind the accelerated learning model.

As I write, some highly topical and somewhat unusual research on the visual and spatial capacities of London taxi-cab drivers' brains has gained media attention. According to the scientists, sites within the brain that contribute to visual and spatial recall are more highly developed in individuals who, for a living, have to use such functions on a daily basis. Taxi drivers with 40 years of experience have greater neural density within sites of the hippocampus devoted to spatial organisation and recall than does the average member of the public.

I cannot say whether or not this report is true. It does seem to support a number of our underlying principles for accelerated learning. It is a case of 'use it or lose it' and, following Hebb, "cells that fire together, survive together and wire together". What's more, "our capacity for visual and spatial recall is potentially enormous". For taxi-cab drivers, not only does this mean that they have accurate recall of their ultimate destination, but know the most circuitous route with which to get you there! For our learners, it again reminds us of the benefit of tapping into the enormous human capacity for visual and spatial organisation.

Reading *MapWise* reminded me of the Milnathort paradox. The paradox goes like this. We'll describe Milnathort as a very small town. It contains a few shops, a restaurant, a Post Office, a Town Clock on top of a Town Hall and a dispersed settlement of houses. A family – let's call them the Smalls – decide to travel the 15 or so miles to Milnathort to eat at a restaurant. They have to come down through a circuitous route across the hills to get there. As they travel along the narrow roads there is a little desultory conversation, but the mood is generally apathetic. The meal is taken in much the same way with the grandparents quiet and disapproving, the mother harassed and tired, the father distracted and the children restless and bored. Soon they are driving back, listless, disappointed and finding it hard to hide their frustration. 'Well we only went to please you', say the grandparents; 'We only agreed to go because the children like it', say the parents; 'We never wanted to go there – who said that we like it?' say the children. It transpires that each individual had been second-guessing the motives of all the others. Assumptions had been made but not tested. Clarity had been replaced with obfuscation. Conformity had displaced individual need. The result was that they all ended up where they didn't want, or need, to be. The lesson is, if you don't want to end up in Milnathort, test assumptions, check for understanding, surface and connect your thinking. *MapWise* offers a medium for doing so.

Where learning outcomes and routes to those outcomes are considered and shared, then understanding is deliberately surfaced. In such a climate, learning is transformed. We share our thinking and our understanding firstly with ourselves and then with others. It is done through language: the language of the teacher and the language of the learner. It is also done through visual and spatial representation. The value of *MapWise* is that it offers a medium for surfacing understanding, which combines both.

MapWise, like all other books in the *Accelerated Learning Series,* is distinct. It attempts to model the practices it espouses. It is transparent, not only in its ideas and how they can be used but where these ideas originate. Its medium is also its message. It demonstrates the quality of metacognition and invites you to make your own connections. The tools described and demonstrated throughout *MapWise* encourage connectivity. It is connectivity which takes us out of the realm of creating visual images and into the possibility of developing and extending thinking. A good chess player not only remembers the look of the pieces and the positions on the board but also can readily envisage the connective possibilities inherent in each combination of moves. Anyone with a good memory can remember the look of and the spatial location of the pieces. This does not make you a grandmaster. In everyday life and in the classroom, exposure and rehearsal of novel information is not enough. It is only when connectivity is emphasised in our everyday maps of the world that recall improves and our quality of understanding is enhanced.

In front of me I have a new 50 pence coin. Most of us encounter these coins on a daily basis. Can you describe the coin? Can you do so accurately? Could you draw the coin? A 50 pence coin has at least six distinguishing features. It has seven sides. On one face the figure of Britannia looks to the right over the number 50 and is surrounded by the words 'FIFTY PENCE'. On the other, a representation of the Queen facing right and surrounded by the words 'ELIZABETH II D G REG F D 1998'. In a modest research project, 95% of adults asked to draw both sides failed to get all six features. Most could only get two features. Estimates of the number of sides varied between three and eight! When shown 12 possible drawings to choose from, fewer than half got the correct one.

So what? Simple exposure to phenomena does not guarantee recall. We use these coins every day, yet we cannot remember what they look like. Nor does it seem that frequency of exposure significantly improves recall. What might make a difference is to deliberately – almost self-consciously – require attention to be directed in a specific way; to 'draw attention' in a different way. When participants were asked to deliberately look at and then visually record the detail of the coin and, having done so, explain their outcomes to someone else, their recall improved dramatically. When this method was rehearsed over a spaced period, recall was 100%. The methods in *MapWise* help teachers and their learners to 'draw attention'. Drawing attention requires more than visual recall: it requires an underlying conceptual understanding.

Stephen Pinker neatly epitomises our argument when he says, "Visual thinking is often driven more strongly by the conceptual knowledge we use to organise our images than by the contents of the images themselves". He goes on to say that, "at some point between gazing and thinking, images must give way to ideas" (*How the Mind Works*, by Stephen Pinker, Penguin, 1997, page 298).

MapWise is a challenging book. It looks good but is not about being good looking. It uses language, but suggests that language can bury or surface thought. It provides very detailed information, but suggests that information is redundant unless it is connected to other information. It is not about art, but represents itself through striking visual data. I invite you to accept the *MapWise* challenge and would therefore wish to draw *your* attention to the very powerful tools it provides.

Alistair Smith
Accelerated Learning Series General Editor
April 2000

The inside story

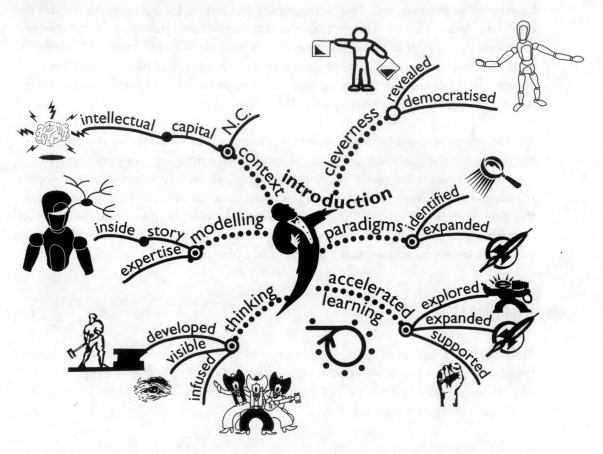

Perhaps the best way to illustrate what can be achieved using *MapWise* is to borrow some key phrases from David Blunkett, United Kingdom Minister for Education, and Carol McGuiness, author of the DfEE's report *From thinking skills to thinking schools*…

MapWise "is about the ability to analyse and make connections, to use knowledge effectively, to solve problems and to think creatively" (1). It is based around a technique called model mapping – a "theory of cognition, which sees learners as active creators of their knowledge and frameworks of interpretation".

"Teaching thinking skills not only makes children more intelligent, it raises standards of achievement."

Michael Barber, Times Educational Supplement, May 1999

"Learning is about searching out meaning and imposing structure … It equips students to go beyond the information given, to deal systematically yet flexibly with novel problems and situations, to adopt a critical attitude to information and argument, as well as to communicate effectively … If students are to become better thinkers – to learn meaningfully, to think flexibly and to make reasoned judgements – then they must be taught explicitly how to do it."

Through model mapping, *MapWise* does exactly this – it shows how to help students become better thinkers, and thus 'democratises' cleverness. Model mapping ensures that tasks will always "have a degree of open-endedness and uncertainty to permit learners to impose meaning or to make judgements or to produce multiple solutions". Model mapping enables learners "to make their own thought processes more explicit"; it ensures that "talking about thinking – questioning, predicting, contradicting, doubting – is not only tolerated but actively pursued" (2).

The Government of the United Kingdom is piloting schemes to develop the skills highlighted in the quotation marks above – the skills of thinking. They are doing this seemingly unaware that model mapping – a highly satisfactory approach to developing thinking skills – is already with us and has been in use for over 20 years. By the end of this book you should see that the claims made in this book about what can be achieved through model mapping are not exaggerated, nor are they particularly ambitious. By the end of the book you will see that they are, in fact, obvious.

◆ The inside story

This book gives you access to the 'inside story' of your own thinking and your students' learning. The book is not about what people say or do, but rather what happens that enables them to say or do it. By looking beneath the surface, you can create a uniquely powerful leverage for your teaching.

It is not necessarily easy to explain to others how you do what you do. Even when very skilled people are highly motivated, and indeed paid, to tell others how they achieve what they achieve, they mostly fail to do so; witness, the failure of the new Advanced Skill Teachers to articulate to others how they excel at teaching. The national educational press carried the headline "Teaching Wisdom that Stays Silent" (*Times Educational Supplement*, 3/9/99)

with a sub-heading declaring "The best teachers cannot discuss their skills, a survey of 'master craftsmen and women' has found" (3). The studies on which the report was based were carried out in the United States and the United Kingdom and concluded that "… the efficient exploitation of [teachers'] excellence is denied to their colleagues and to their school systems. They are potentially one of the most precious resources in the whole educational enterprise – and they cannot be used." It seems that there is not yet an awareness of the need, let alone an agreed technology, for the explanation and demonstration of interior learning processes – the 'inside story'.

◆ Intention of the book

Model mapping has been available for a long time, though you may know it by other names, such as 'mind mapping' or 'memory mapping'. Using this technique, you are able to produce models of your thoughts about a particular concept or idea – hence the name 'model mapping'. *MapWise* shows how model mapping can be used as the most powerful accelerated learning technique available for both teachers and learners. It is the first book that demonstrates how model mapping can be used to

- ◆ teach thinking skills as part of subject delivery
- ◆ support each stage of the accelerated learning process
- ◆ demonstrate and develop intelligence
- ◆ develop four essential learning skills that all learners need – irrespective of their preferred learning style
- ◆ transform the teaching and learning systems in operation in classrooms.

Ultimately *MapWise* will support you in helping your students to understand themselves and the world around them, both at school and beyond. *MapWise* is intended to increase both your own and your students' capacity for learning.

◆ Accelerated learning

Accelerated learning is about learning how to learn. It places emphasis on developing stimulating environments and positive personal states in order to optimise learning. Accelerated learning was once merely a minority interest of those looking for cutting edge approaches to actualising human potential, but it is at last mainstream and making an impact on thousands of students in schools up and down the country. Even the Government (4) is now advocating accelerated learning techniques to teachers and head teachers.

Through accelerated learning, teachers have developed an arsenal of strategies that are tuned to the needs of the learner. They are now rethinking their approaches to teaching in the light of what research tells us about how our brains work. They are aiming to manage the learning process in order to maximise students' ability to access the content of the curriculum.

With this light shining clearly on learners' needs, the self-esteem of students and their positive outlook on learning are inevitably blossoming. The outcome of learners' new curiosity about themselves is, naturally enough, an improvement in academic results. Focusing on the process of learning in this way is raising standards.

◆ Learning how to learn

It is interesting to note, however, that while teachers *are* now focusing on the 'process of learning', this term has not so far included any models of, or strategies for, the actual processes of thinking and learning that occur within the learner's mind. Schools have learned how to design visually stimulating environments, how to create safe and challenging cultures, how to foster self-esteem, how to deliver material in multi-sensory ways and in a brain-friendly sequence, how to engage the learner's memory, how to meet the learner's physiological needs, and even how to integrate ambient music into learning. All these strategies are a tremendous boost to the learner and make learning more likely to happen. But these strategies do not tell us what learning actually *is* or how it occurs. They therefore comprise only part of what is involved in the well-worn phrase 'learning how to learn'.

In short, it is currently not strictly accurate to say that accelerated learning is about 'learning how to learn'. A more accurate description might be 'learning how to make learning more likely'. When asked what they mean by 'learning how to learn', colleagues' answers relate to the conditions of learning. The phrase itself has such a comforting, even inspiring, feel to it that it sometimes seems that merely to repeat it will produce benefits and insights; witness, its inclusion in the new National Curriculum. It is mentioned but not explained or illustrated.

It is time this phrase was examined – that the 'inside story' was investigated. There is still a missing set of tools that can do for the mind what accelerated learning has already done for the environment, culture, and psycho-physical state of the learner. Now we are able to see the effects that 'external' conditions can have on learning, we are ready to consider the impact that cognitive tools can have on the process of learning itself.

How much better would results be if learners, in addition to experiencing stimulating environments and positive personal states, also had a tool that gave them access to the very structure of their thinking and learning? What if all learners had a technique that could be used to develop their thinking skills? What if all learners knew how to generate ideas, organise concepts, ensure recall and model the thinking of subject specialists? And what if this technology was fun to use, very individualised and easily communicable? Furthermore, what if it was of equal benefit to teachers in their planning, teaching and assessment of students' understanding?

◆ Modelling the learning process

This is where an understanding of the 'inside story' is needed. In addition to, and beyond, describing the external factors that impact on learning, we must examine what goes on in our heads when we learn, when we think effectively, and when we master skills.

This enquiry is fascinating. What do we do in our minds when we experience the sensations associated with understanding? What is it that we are *not* doing when we experience the sensations associated with not understanding something? From a teaching perspective, how can we share with students and colleagues our ability to understand the subjects that we teach? How can we most effectively communicate how we reached this level of understanding?

Oliver remembers an occasion when he was frustrated by his unsuccessful attempts to teach someone how to catch a frisbee. Repeatedly waiting for his friend to retrieve the frisbee was becoming tiresome.

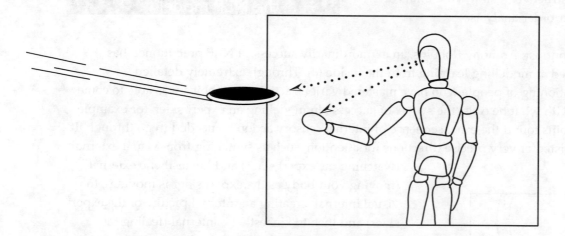

Abandoning all the established, but unsuccessful, teaching strategies he knew, Oliver started to really look at what he was doing when he caught the frisbee himself. This close scrutiny produced an altogether different teaching approach. He realised that all his friend needed to do was to capture visually, as in a 'mental photograph', the very instant when the frisbee indented into the stretched skin between thumb and index finger. There was to be no attempt to catch the frisbee, simply to witness in great detail and 'slow motion', this split-second instant. When doing this, and not attempting to do anything else, the friend caught the frisbee – repeatedly.

A few years later, sports coach Timothy Gallwey published his books on *The Inner Game*. These books took a similar approach to learning and achievement. By getting at the 'inside story', success was achieved through accurate modelling of the learning process. So the question is 'what do we *do* when we learn?' not in terms of what the environment looks like and what behaviours we display, but in terms of what is going on inside our minds.

◆ Neuro Linguistic Programming

The authors are not alone in their passion for modelling the origins of excellence; the very basis of NLP (Neuro Linguistic Programming) is predicated on this intention. Developed in the 1970s, this psychology continues to be a central pillar of accelerated learning. We can learn much from its successes – and failures.

In her book on NLP and learning (5), Dianne Beaver looks at modelling successful learners. She goes about this by modelling what she can see – behaviour. Much to her consternation, the best students in the class exhibited the worst physical states for learning. They slouched, breathed shallowly, frowned, and worried over their work! This failure is instructive. It shows the limits of lower order analysis.

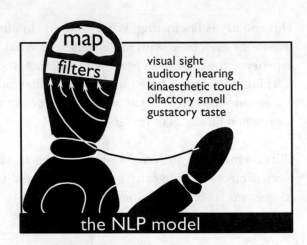

visual sight
auditory hearing
kinaesthetic touch
olfactory smell
gustatory taste

the NLP model

By contrast, Anthony Robbins, an extraordinarily successful NLP practitioner, has looked at modelling learning from the inside (6). Through extremely detailed questioning of people who have mastered various activities, Robbins was able to come up with what he calls 'the syntax of success'. In modelling an expert skier, for example, Robbins found the exact sequence of internal sensory action he needed to go through. It consisted of very precise directions for attention, such as switching from visual external (watching the expert skier) and kinaesthetic external (moving your body as the expert skier is moving), to visual internal (creating an internal picture of the expert skier) and then to kinaesthetic internal (feeling the sensation of moving without actually moving).

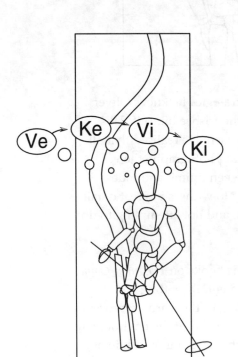

The sequence continues, but this much gives a sense of the possibility of entering into the same mental landscape as those you are modelling. It is this ability to access internal terrains that gives model mapping such potential for transforming learning. What is going on in the terrain that we call our mind? How can we see the 'inside story'?

◆ Expanding the paradigm

It has not always been apparent the magnitude or power of the role that model mapping could have. Model mapping has for too long been narrowly defined. It has been caught within the confines of a 'new age' study method. Its central appearance in such mildly bizarre events as the Mind Olympics has confirmed its peripheral status in mainstream education. It was only a few years ago that Oliver, who has been mapping for over 20 years, realised the increased potential mapping has for understanding learning. In Alistair Smith and Nicola Call's book, *Accelerated Learning in Primary Schools* (7), he gives an account of his realisation.

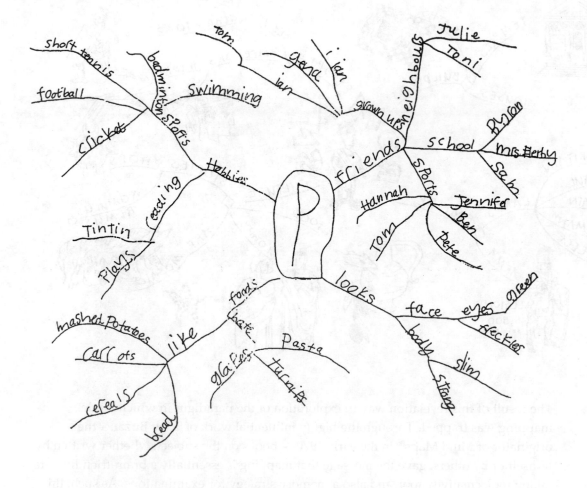

Oliver has a son, Pascal, who has Down's syndrome. Only when his son, then at a mainstream primary school, was described by his class teacher as merely 'barking at print' in his attempts to read did Oliver start to use mapping other than for taking and making notes for himself. By asking Pascal to place words and pictures of the central themes of a book into specific locations on a blank page, Oliver started to map Pascal's understanding of the book. Further distinctions within the developing map revealed another level of understanding that linear text or verbal format would have left undiscovered. The map had externalised Pascal's understanding and, having been made concrete and visual, it stimulated further discussion and learning.

Far from being an ordeal, this initial mapping experience was fun and both father and son enjoyed it. Mapping became a very supportive prop for Pascal's continued learning and understanding. When any topic from school needed explaining, out came the A3 paper and coloured felt tips!

For Pascal, mapping had brought wisdom; he had become 'MapWise'. He started to use maps in other ways. When he had to give a five-minute talk to his classmates on the Romans, he used a map his father had drawn to guide and support him.

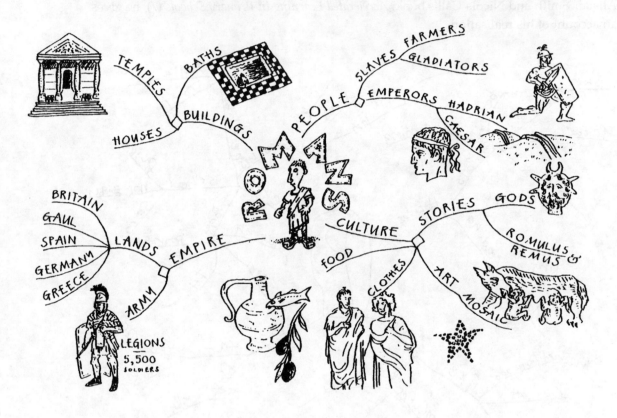

The result of this revelation was an exploration of the paradigm in which model mapping was trapped. Through the highly influential work of Tony Buzan – the originator of Mind Maps® in the early 1970s – books on the subject, whether written by himself or by others, gave the message that mapping is essentially a brain-friendly note-taking tool, creativity tool, and also a memory strategy for examinations. As such, this was a tremendous contribution. The authors' own experience, however, indicates that this 'definition' has limited the potential impact of mapping on learning in the classroom. *MapWise* shows you how to explore and fully realise this potential.

◆ Compelling reasons

The emphasis of this book is to show how model mapping can 'democratise' cleverness by literally showing us what it looks like. It can externalise the internal and organised thinking of clever people, which is the basis for their effective decisions and actions. If thinking is spread out onto a map, understanding can be both communicated and developed. Translating rapid, private, ephemeral and abstract thinking into static, public, concrete and accessible demonstrations reveals concepts to all learners.

Essentially, then, model mapping supports teachers' explanations and learners' understanding. The qualities of model mapping that are brought to the fore in *MapWise*, in addition to the established benefits of left–right brain laterality promoted by Tony Buzan, should make model mapping irresistible to schools.

As far back as 1982, a series of books entitled *I See What You Mean* (8) outlined very clearly the compelling benefits of modelling knowledge graphically. Modelling – producing graphical or pictorial representations of knowledge – requires thorough comprehension and understanding of the material under scrutiny. Underlying structures and organising principles must be identified and the learner finds herself taking an

active and creative part in processing the information. Because understanding is engaged, and the outcome is a unique visual portrayal of this understanding, memory is greatly enhanced. Any lack of clarity literally shows up in the portrayal. The student who is able to model her understanding can truly claim to be a model learner.

MapWise aims to provoke you to consider why you are not yet providing this invaluable tool to your students. By the end of the book, it is hoped, you will be convinced to take action. By completing the step-by-step instructions, you will become accomplished in creating model maps. By integrating model maps into your teaching, you and your students will become 'MapWise'. Quite simply, you will be expanding your students' capacity for learning.

◆ Signposts to the chapters

The book is set out in the following way to help you to become 'MapWise'.

Chapter 1 — Maps

This chapter looks at the place and function of maps. It looks at maps in general, and the specific aspects that constitute a map. The history and descriptions of model mapping are traced out. Model maps are deconstructed to reveal their essential nature and structure.

Chapter 2 — How to map

Step-by-step instructions, from exercises in categorisation to examples of design formats, take you from complete novice to accomplished mapper.

Chapter 3 — Teaching mapping

Various ways of teaching mapping to students are described.

Chapter 4 — Thinking skills

An overview of the implementation of thinking skills in schools is given. Arguments for both separate thinking skills programmes and subject integration are detailed. The role that model mapping can play as the resolution to this dilemma is explained.

Chapter 5 — Teaching and learning systems

The way in which model mapping can be both the catalyst for, and the tool of, an interactive loop between teacher and student is explained. The limitation of a linear delivery model of teaching is compared to one where both teacher and learner become interdependent learners.

Chapter 6 — Maps in the classroom

The way model mapping supports both the learner and the teacher at each stage of the accelerated learning cycle is examined. Benefits described elsewhere in the book are applied practically.

Chapter 7 — Cleverness and internal maps

The phenomenon of 'being clever' is explored. The process of sharing cleverness is explained.

◆ <u>Maps</u>

charting their history, value, function, design and applications

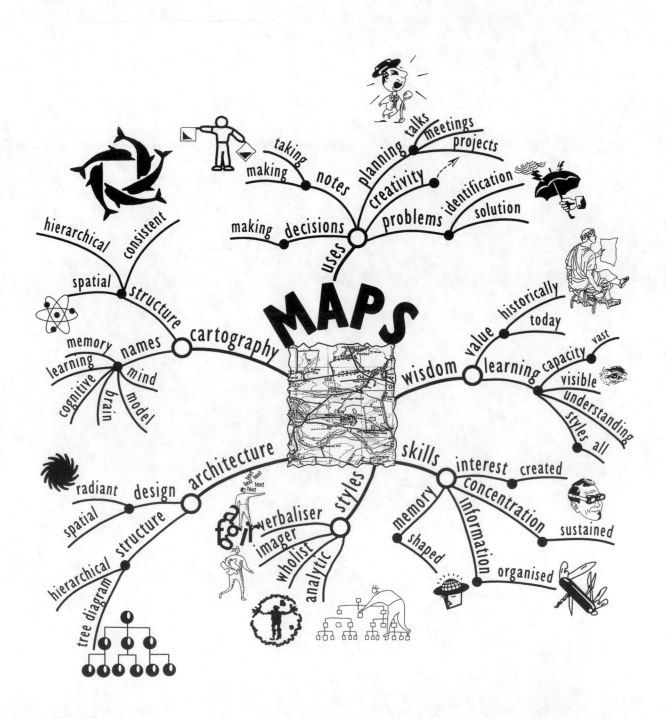

Chapter 1

Maps

charting their history, value, function, design and applications

COMING SOON!

1 How the use of maps, throughout history, has been associated with power.
2 Why visual thinking is the most effective and powerful way of learning.
3 The keys to understanding the organisation and structure of information.
4 Why this book is relevant to all learners, irrespective of perceived learning style preference.
5 How this book can be used to develop the four essential learning skills.
6 Why model mapping has as many applications as linear text, if not more.

The standard forms of communications we use can be seen as maps. They enable us to get beyond our own ideas to those of others. They enable us to find new information. We trade our perceptions and ideas through the currency of maps … A map is anything that shows you the way from one point to another, from one level of understanding to another.

Richard Saul Wurman (1)

The BBC television series *Blackadder Goes Forth* is set during the First World War. In one episode, Colonel Melchett asks his aid, Captain Darling, for a map of the Western Front: "At ease everybody. Now, where's my map. Come on."

Darling hands Melchett the map, who opens it up on the desk. Melchett comments to Darling, "It's a barren featureless desert out there, isn't it", to which Darling responds, "It's the other side sir".

21

Maps are – if you know how to use them – very useful. Had Colonel Melchett had access to *MapWise*, this chapter would have helped him get the most out of using maps. It is divided up into the following sections.

- ◆ The wisdom of maps
- ◆ Cognitive cartography
- ◆ Information architecture
- ◆ Stylish learning
- ◆ The bottom line
- ◆ Use it or lose it

◆ The wisdom of maps

Maps are not a recent invention. They have a history of centuries and – as the cave paintings of early humans and the hieroglyphics of ancient Egypt illustrate – visual note-taking has been around for even longer (2).

The use and availability of maps has played a crucial part in the unfolding of history. As the Europeans took over North America, maps were used to carve up the Indian Territories; the Treaty of Versailles saw Europe literally redrawn; and again following the Second World War, Europe was divided between East and West. Throughout history, in fact, maps have always been equated with power, whether they depicted hunting grounds, military sites, trade routes or buried treasure (1). Maps had value and were prized.

In another episode of *Blackadder Goes Forth*, Lieutenant George and Captain Blackadder are sent on a night patrol to draw the German trenches. As they are crawling around in the mud Captain Blackadder asks Lieutenant George, "Where the hell are we?"

George (looking at the map): Well it's a bit difficult to say. We appear to have crawled into an area marked with mushrooms.

Blackadder: What do those symbols denote?

George: That we are in a field of mushrooms?

Blackadder: Lieutenant – that is a military map. It is unlikely to list interesting flora and fungi. Look at the key and you'll discover that those mushrooms aren't for picking.

George: Good Lord you're quite right, Sir. It says 'mine'. So, these mushrooms must belong to the man who made the map!

We can draw several useful lessons from this. First, the ability to read and understand maps can be an enriching (and in Lieutenant George's case life-saving) experience. Second, maps show an individual's, a group's, or an organisation's mental *representation* of an area of territory – they are *not*, however, the territory itself. The fact that Melchett did not realise that he was looking at the wrong side of the map (page 21) suggests, perhaps, how unfamiliar the generals were with the reality of warfare in the trenches. These two examples serve to illustrate the usefulness of being able to read and understand maps.

Today it is unlikely that we will be using maps to look for buried treasure, follow trade routes or manoeuvre around hunting grounds. But maps continue to reveal treasures. Contemporary treasures may be less dramatic and often more abstract, but they remain things that we value. We now live in an age centred on knowledge; information is the backdrop for, and the very substance of, many of our endeavours. The treasure we seek is *knowledge* and the subsequent meaning we can create from it.

Maps can play a crucial part in finding our treasure – revealing knowledge and encouraging confidence. It is just unfortunate, perhaps, that our contemporary treasure is not perceived as being as glamorous as buried bullion.

Some people doubt that any topic can be mapped. What of the arts, for example? Surely there are some areas that are too subtle to be the subject of this cartographic analysis. Well, there can be no more subtle area than that of human consciousness and this has been successfully 'mapped'.

> "[Maps] can make sense of chaos, define the abstract with the concrete, and generally act as weapons by which we can subdue complex ideas and unruly numbers. Well-crafted maps can reduce anxiety."
>
> *Richard Saul Wurman (1)*

> "I needed maps, and each of these traditions [eastern religions] had its own to offer. At various times each of these maps has helped me find my way in meditation or made me feel safe in unfamiliar territory."
>
> *Daniel Goleman (3)*

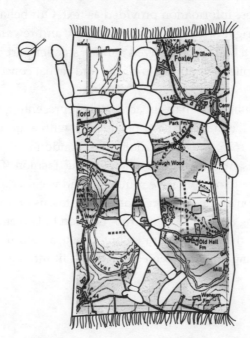

The constraints of linear presentation

Linear orientation of information dominates our lives, because we read and write in lines of text that – in western cultures – we follow from left-to-right. Let us consider what we do with the information that we read in this left-to-right fashion. As we finish one page and turn to the next, we have to store the essential information of the first page in our memory. Of course, we are not conscious that we do this but if we did not the next page would be meaningless since it would have nothing to link with or hook in to. Furthermore, we do not store the information in a linear sequence, since each new piece of information in a book does not necessarily refer to the piece immediately preceding it. Instead, the reader is constantly asked to link new information to old information that may have been read several pages before.

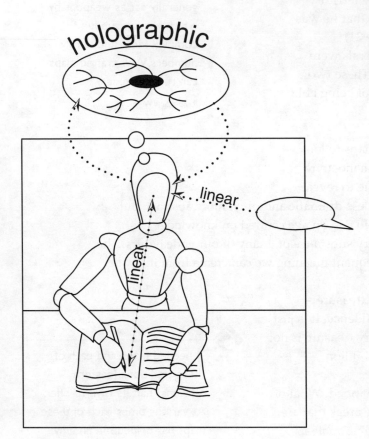

So, we take information from linear text and process it in a non-linear way. It is not, perhaps, surprising that a significant number of people have difficulty doing this, given the complexity of the task.

The reading example illustrates that we do not think in a linear way. This means that, since the development of writing, humans have had to impose upon themselves a continual behaviour modification programme in order to process information provided as text. Our behaviour has been shaped by the linear, left-to-right orientation of written text, and rewards have gone to those who master this format. Maps have played a much smaller part in our communication systems despite their ability to clarify and reveal concepts.

Another example of the usefulness of maps in accurately representing the way we think can be shown by comparing the map on the opposite page with a modern road map. The map opposite, drawn in 1675, shows the route from London to Dover in a linear way, while a road map represents the route in a holographic fashion. The linear map gives no means of working out an alternative route if a road is closed. Travelling by this map gives you little indication of the location of any other towns or areas of interest. Its function is limited to showing a singular route from London to Dover. This obviously fulfils the purpose for which the map was drawn but, unlike a road map, it gives you no support at all in understanding how the elements within it fit into the surrounding area.

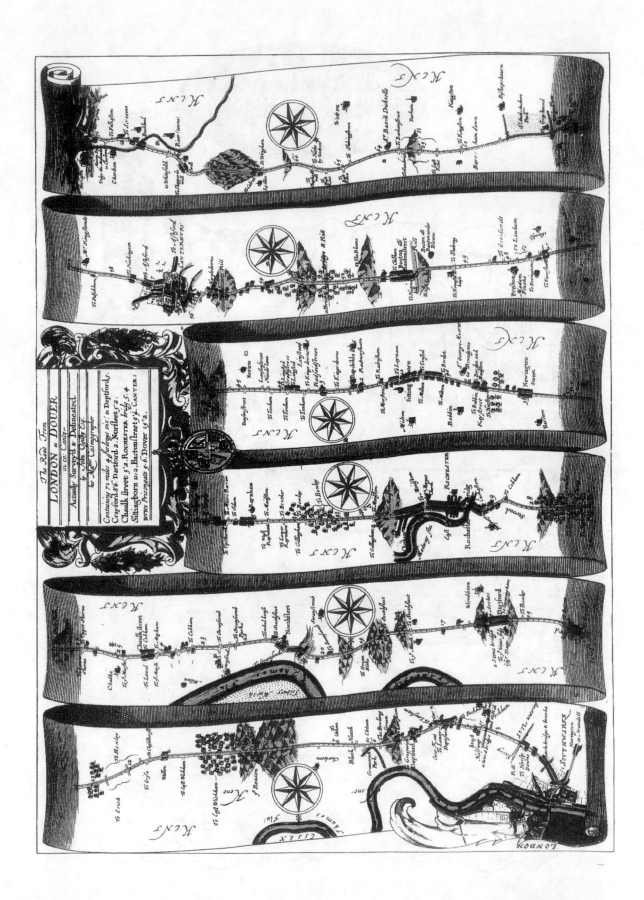

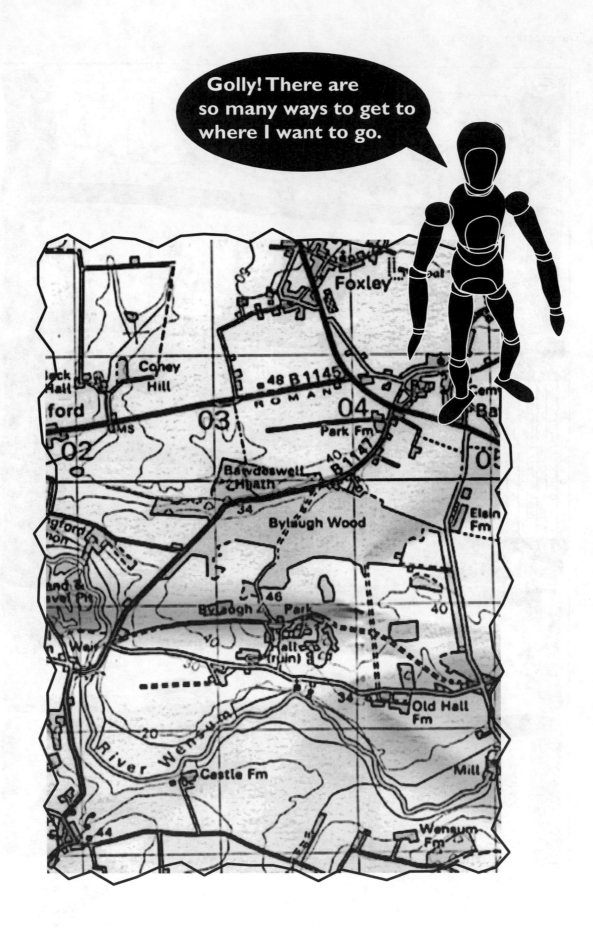

MAPWISE — accelerated learning through visible thinking

The experience of many children in the classroom can be likened to following the linear map from London to Dover. They are given information bit by bit in a linear fashion but they may not be supported in working out how it all fits together. What's more, the danger when using a linear route is that if children lose their way, they may never get back on track.

By presenting information outside of the constraints of a linear mode, maps offer the reader not just the information depicted in each section of the map, but also the relationships between the sections. The total knowledge gained exemplifies the notion that the whole is more than the sum of its parts (4).

"Most people have a fairly limited concept of a map as a depiction of a particular geographic location. To find our way through information, we also rely on maps that will tell us where we are in relation to the information, give us a sense of perspective, and enable us to make comparisons between information."

Richard Saul Wurman (1)

Another analogy demonstrating the constraints of communicating information in a linear way is provided by digital watches. These are the equivalent of linear text; information is given in discrete, independent packets. The exact time of the present moment is shown, but no more is on offer.

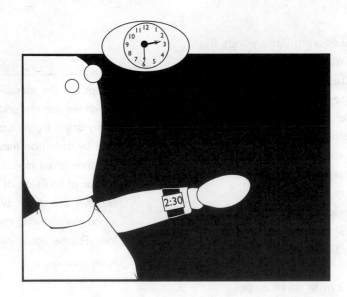

With an analogue watch, the positions of the hands signify the exact current time *as well as* more tacit knowledge – they also form a relationship with the other points of the watch, so the observer gains an additional sense of the current time in relation to other times. For example, if the time is half past two, then the position of the hands in relation to the numerals 4 and 5 will tacitly inform the wearer that she has only one hour to complete her tasks before preparing for a meeting scheduled at a quarter to five. This information is tacit – nowhere on the watch does it state this. It is also immediate – no time is taken to assimilate the information.

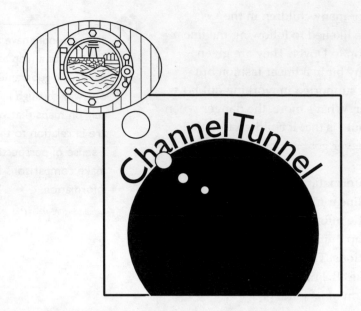

Similarly, we could say that the journey from the UK to France via the channel tunnel is equivalent to a 'digital' experience, while travel by sea is analogue. The tunnel offers a limited vision and therefore experience. By contrast, during the sea journey different perspectives will offer more scope for meaning, which is usually interpreted as being more enjoyable.

Wurman (1) makes a similar analogy in contrasting a plane journey that follows a straight line (digital), with a pedestrian journey that involves, by necessity, a more circuitous route (analogue). Getting lost is always a possibility with the 'analogue' walk, though with a map you can see how to get back on course. A 'digital' plane journey more-or-less guarantees your arrival at the destination – as long as you don't fall out!

"Maps are the metaphoric means by which we can understand and act upon information from outside sources. A map by definition must perform, whether it is a multimillion dollar, four-colour production of the national weather system or two cans of beer on a counter showing the relationship of a friend's new house to his old one."

Richard Saul Wurman (1)

As Lieutenant George and Colonel Melchett illustrate beautifully (page 21), reading maps requires some degree of training, otherwise the wealth of information within them can confuse rather than simplify. You can get lost. Initially it may seem strange that any training is needed as "… many users [of maps] would maintain that using a map should require no more than normal vision and average intelligence" (4). However, compared to the number of years spent in educating students to use linear means of communicating, the proposition of teaching them to read maps seems reasonable.

"Trying to wade through information without a sense of structure is like going to the Library of Congress and aimlessly combing the shelves for a particular book. Once you have a sense of how the whole is organised, you will reduce the frustration of searching for a needle in a haystack. Even if the needle is all that you need, it will behove you to know how the hay is organised."

Richard Saul Wurman (1)

Readers of maps need to understand how the map is constructed. The very nature of the construction gives meaning to the content. Different types of maps have different methods of organisation. The organisation of some types is more evident than that of others. Later in the book, in chapter 2, the organising principles of model maps will be explained. We look now at an aspect of maps that distinguishes them from text – images.

Using images

We have a need to look for patterns. Schools do not abandon visual learning entirely – they simply do not spend much time teaching it. If you reflect on the fact that "The way we learn, and subsequently remember, bears a strong relationship to the way our senses operate", it becomes clear that "we, as educators, cannot afford to ignore the fact that a very high proportion of all sensory learning is visual" (5). The design and use of visual learning techniques, and opportunities for their use, should carry a higher priority in education and would benefit from extended research (6). Alistair Smith and Nicola Call (7) argue strongly to reconsider the current lack of emphasis placed on visual learning:

"Perhaps our natural disposition towards organising information in our heads through visual patterns and spatial relationships is undervalued. In arguing for the teaching and the use of mapping techniques we are arguing for the extension of the visual and spatial propensity that seems an inherent part of our neural architecture. We are all mappers."

Our capacity for visual recall is astonishing. Recently, Ian recovered a store of his old comics that had been in his father's attic for over 20 years. This is how he described looking at them again. "I was acutely aware, as I went from one front cover to the next, that none of them surprised me. I went through over a thousand comics and each and every one was familiar to me. As I read through a few comic strips it was the pictures not the words that took me back to my childhood. On one front cover of a 'Tiger and Scorcher' comic Billy Dane was playing cricket … and his cricket bat, because of the angle it was drawn at, seemed shorter than a real bat. This picture took me back to the chair by the stove in my Grandparents' house where I had been when I first read the story. Without thinking I recalled what my Grandmother was cooking at the time – I could smell the stew and dumplings – where my Grandad had been that morning and my confusion at why the artist had drawn such a short bat."

"We don't 'see' with our eyes at all, but we see with our brain."

Harry Alder and Beryl Heather (8)

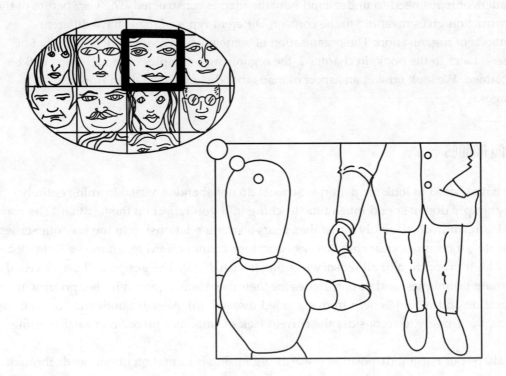

How many times have you heard people say 'I never forget a face'? When you bump into an old acquaintance or ex-colleague, what do you remember first – the face or the name? The experiments of Haber (9) in the early 1970s revealed that we have a nearly perfect recall of images. Eventually viewing over 2500 images at a rate of one per second, participants in Haber's visual experiment achieved an accuracy of recall of between 85% and 95%.

Images provide such strong, stimulating and memorable hooks for memory. We readily internalise images, and are able to recall minor details within them. This "… capacity to internalise and manipulate visual images is a powerful one which some researchers have gone on to link to a stage in our evolutionary development. The ability to locate and move from a source of threat, or to visually map the position of traps, or to direct oneself back to a herd of migrating beasts would help our ancestors survive" (7). It is no surprise, then, that images have continued to be an inherent part of maps.

"[Students] had better recall of short abstract prose passages when they were illustrated by one complex picture than by four simple ones of separate components of the story."

J. R. Lewin, L. K. Schriberg and J. K. Berry (10)

Building on the visual skills of recall, we can add the visual skills of interpretation. Maps of all sorts make use of visual devices that save space, time and effort. We call these 'symbols' or 'icons'.

Icons offer a likeness of the object portrayed, whereas symbols have only an agreed and abstract relationship with the object designated (4). You could say that icons 'reproduce' while symbols 'stand for'. It is possible, of course, for an icon to be so stylised as to appear to have little or no resemblance to the object. We could, therefore, draw a continuum from perfect visual representation to abstract, arbitrarily agreed relationship. This latter end of the continuum gives the cartographer, the map maker, the ability to represent quite abstract items; even emotions can be represented in this way. Existing visual languages already do this and are available to map makers. For example, children at Woodlands Special School in Chelmsford use Makaton (12) symbols as part of their maps. Nancy Margulies (13), author and presenter of mind mapping materials, supports her readers and gives them confidence in their map making using a symbol system called SymbolVision. Fellow mind map author Joyce Wycoff (14) suggests using a set of quite common symbols to stand for abstract notions, such as a downward pointing arrow standing for 'less, fewer, decreasing'.

"[Students] spontaneously produced mental imagery, whether they were reading poems, stories or expository texts, and … the students' interest in what they read increased with the amount of imagery they reported."

S. A. Long, P. N. Winograd and C. A. Bridge (11)

Symbols make it possible to present a great deal of information on a map in a very effective, space-efficient way. Consider the information contained within one page of a street map book. How many pages of text would it take to present the same information? Other types of maps, too, can be used to communicate in this compact, accessible way.

The spatial grouping of symbols on maps offers another level of information, beyond the meanings of the symbols themselves. It has even been said (13) that a map as a whole is itself an icon. So, not only are the separate details (icons and symbols) visually memorable, but the very shape of the map itself can be remembered easily. While linear text can often look 'all the same', maps always have a unique quality about them. Again, research has emphasised the power of visual recall: in an experiment that pursued and developed the findings of Haber (9), Nickerson (15) presented his subjects with vivid and striking pictures – 10,000 in total at a rate of 600 per minute! The results are astounding. Subjects, tested immediately after their presentation, achieved an average 98% accuracy of recall.

◆ Cognitive cartography

We have seen that maps are visually very effective, which partly explains the current increasing awareness of the potential of maps as a tool for learning. Now let us explore the development of the use of maps in education.

Over the last 25 years, there have been many developments in the creation and use of maps for understanding, learning, communication and memory. Some of the maps developed have distinct differences in form and function. Others are more similar than their creators might care to admit.

In 1974, Buzan published his book *Use Your Head* (16) in which Mind Maps® were presented. In the book, which was an enormous contribution to learning, Buzan explained how he was frustrated with the complete lack of information given to learners about their brain and how it worked. He illustrated the limited benefits of advanced note-taking in linear format; he then introduced mapping as the effective remedy. Its format was the outcome of his research and personal quest for more effective methods.

In fact, mapping was already in use around that time, albeit for a different purpose. In the late 1960s, Professor Joseph Novak developed what he called Concept Maps™ (20) (see example below). Concept Maps™ have several differences in structure and function

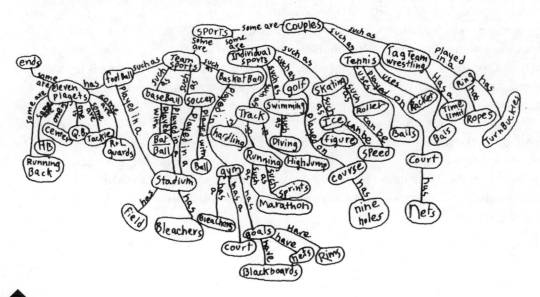

to Mind Maps® (21), but their use of spatial organisation to represent hierarchies of concepts and the idea of using a visual format to illustrate, develop and assess thinking, are features that are central to mapping in general.

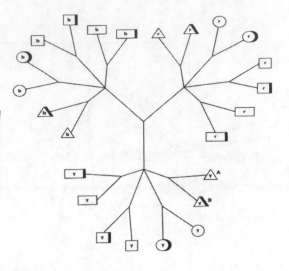

In 1973, Seaborne (17) published a booklet for primary school teachers on how to teach the mathematical thinking involved in the use of sets. The illustration (right) shows the graphic structure used to establish the logical relationships between individual items, and demonstrate the categorisation of objects. In addition, Britton's work of 1970 (19) on language hierarchies covered the same areas, including a link to graphic representation (see example below).

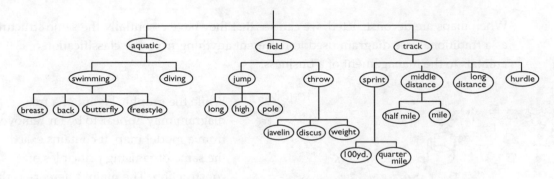

It is not surprising, therefore, that there are many names for mapping, such as 'spider maps', 'spidergrams', 'mubbles', 'clustering', 'brain webs', 'learning maps', 'knowledge maps', 'memory maps' and, of course, 'model maps'. The term 'model maps' is used here because it is the most accurate:

◆ maps are models of our thoughts, not of our minds; a map is not the actual territory, but a model of it

◆ these maps are models of how effective maps can be – they provide good 'role models' for other maps.

Maps themselves have been variously described as

◆ 'a way of hot-wiring your creative juices'

◆ 'multi-handed thought-ball catchers'

◆ 'a Swiss Army Knife for the mind'

◆ 'energising patterns'

◆ 'a way of catching, organising and interpreting thoughts and ideas'

◆ 'a way of putting on paper what's in your head'

◆ 'holographic 'imagisers''

33

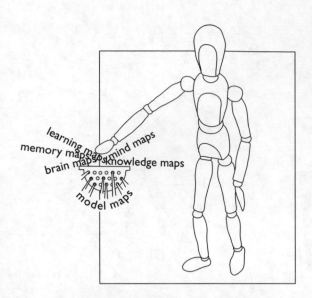

◆ 'doodles with a purpose'

◆ 'mind-mirrors'

◆ 'brain-caring devices'

◆ 'mental volcanoes'

◆ 'multi-ordinate generators'

◆ 'a device for accessing intelligence'

◆ 'goal-centred thought networks'

◆ 'multi-dimensional mnemonic technique'

◆ 'surf boards for the brain'

To make it easy, from here on we shall use the general term 'model mapping' to refer to all variations of mapping.

◆ Information architecture

When maps are deconstructed, we can see that they have essentially the same structure as a traditional tree diagram used to represent anything from the classification of animals to the management of a business.

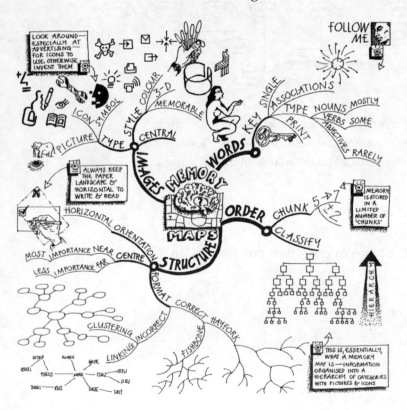

While the graphic layout of a tree diagram may appear to be far removed from a model map, it contains exactly the same organising principles of construction. The main difference is that in a tree diagram, the most significant concept is found at the top with those lower down represented in descending order of importance. In model maps the most important concept is at the centre, with the subordinate concepts radiating to the edges. The two illustrations that follow, for example, shows the same information – at the top of the next page it is shown as a tree diagram (on its side in this case) while on the left it is shown as a model map.

In order to see that these two formats are essentially the same, imagine a tree diagram drawn on paper, with the central concept at the top and the subordinate branches cascading down below it. Now imagine cutting the main subordinate branches off from the main concept, and then cutting between them to separate them. Now you could arrange these subordinate

34

branches around the main concept, instead of below it, and essentially create a model map. The main ideas would be in the centre and the lesser concepts would radiate towards the edge. The illustration below shows a tree diagram chopped up and spread around the main concept – you can see that it is effectively the same as the model map on page 19.

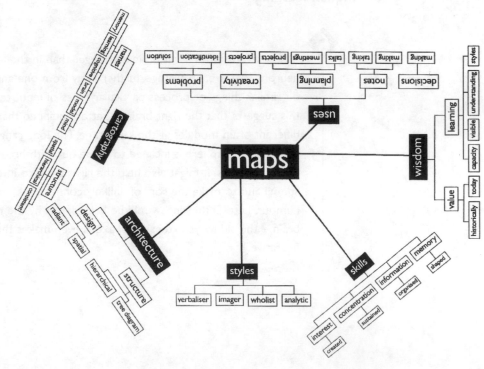

Model maps, like all maps, share this basic organising structure. They may be presented as 'holographic mind projections', likened to the synapses of the brain, described as 'organic thought generators', and so on, but they are fundamentally the same as the classification diagrams used by the Victorians in their quest to analyse and explain the world (19). The rules and conventions of mapping should not disguise or confuse this fact.

What model maps have in contrast to formal tree diagrams is design. This is not to say that they are necessarily artistic in nature. Anybody can construct a model map with the inclusion of images – fine art training is not a requirement. Nor is the belief that you are not a visual learner any sort of real impediment – though more on that later in this chapter (page 38).

Seen from the perspective of design, a model map very largely follows its basic principles of arrangement, balance, colour, dynamism, emphasis, fidelity and graphic harmony (22). Even if that list seems rather daunting, you can see that model maps have the following characteristics, which are totally lacking from linear notes: "visual rhythm, visual pattern, colour, image, visualisation, dimension, spatial awareness, gestalt (wholeness), association" (18).

35

So for the great majority of mappers, artistic considerations are a very minor element. Images are used simply for the fun of creating them and for the serious task of remembering the associations they stimulate. Buzan has encouraged the use of artistic maps, showing many examples in his books as inspiring models to others (18), though Joyce Wycoff sees a limit to the value of the finished products of mapping when she says "No one is ever going to buy your mind maps" (14).

As model maps are visual, it is inevitable that some design or artistic perspective is attributed to them. It is not primarily an artistic distinction that determines their construction, however. It is a balance between the organisational nature of the topic to be mapped and the creativity in finding a spatial structure to represent the conceptual interpretation the mapper has of the topic. Chapter 2 explains exactly what this entails; it is mentioned here simply to emphasise that structures of maps cannot be predetermined. Individuality moulds the nature of the topic under focus. That is why it is not appropriate to offer students a bare map with only the branches drawn, as has been suggested elsewhere.

Maps are models of our thoughts, and so they differ from individual to individual. They represent the way in which our thoughts inter-relate. This matrix of concepts constitutes the meanings we have made of our world. We bring together all our sense impressions and thoughts in this creation, that we can call a schema. 'Schema' is the technical term used by psychologists to describe the construction of our understanding. Chapter 7 examines in detail the development of schemas; here we focus on the fact that the raw data for our schemas come from our total experience of our environment. Because of this, we know that both sides of our brain have been involved.

◆ Stylish learning

"…the axons in the right brain are longer than in the left and this means they connect neurons that are, on average, further away from one another. Given that neurons that do similar things or process particular types of input tend to be clustered together, this suggests that the right brain is better equipped than the left to draw on several different brain modules at the same time. The long-range neural wiring might explain why that hemisphere is inclined to come out with broad, many-faceted, but rather vague concepts. It might also help the right brain to integrate sensory and emotional stimuli and to make the sort of unlikely connections that provide the basis for much humour. 'Lateral thinking' would be helped, too, by the neural arrangement in the right brain – the sideways extension of axons even makes the phrase literal rather than figurative."

Rita Carter (23)

Much has been written about hemispheric learning – how the left and right brain operate. Indeed, much use of this is made to justify the use of model maps. However, Robert Ornstein, winner of the Nobel prize for his discovery of left–right brain differences, comments that the over-simplified way in which his research is interpreted by non-scientists concerns him. Similarly, implying that the connections made on a map are analogous to the synaptic connections in the brain is not strictly appropriate.

There does, however, seem to be agreement that there are certain functions for which the right and left hemispheres of the brain take responsibility. Most significant for us is the agreement that the right brain deals with 'wholeness' or the big picture, whereas the left brain operates at a linear, analytical level of detail.

> "Brain imaging studies confirm that the two hemispheres really do have quite specific skills that are 'hard-wired' to the extent that, in normal circumstances, certain skills will always develop on a particular side … The right hemisphere is also good at grasping wholes, while the left brain likes details … The tasks that each hemisphere takes on are those that fit its style of working: holistic or analytical … They each process their 'halves' of the big picture, and then pool their information."
>
> *Rita Carter (23)*

From the perspective of a teacher, the most important thing is to acknowledge that there is a big picture – a whole – and that there are parts that make up the whole. This may seem obvious, but in fact many schools currently do not teach students 'the big picture'; instead emphasis is on the linear presentation of discrete units of information. Our understanding reflects our ability to place new information inside a bigger picture; model mapping supports the teacher and the learner in doing this because the whole *and* the parts that make up the whole are present at the same time.

As individuals, we have different learning style preferences. Perhaps it is a person's style of thinking and learning that causes differences in the electrical activity of the two sides of his brain (24). There is a plethora of learning style inventories available to use. Educational psychologists Riding and Rayner (25) carried out a major study in this area, looking at data from as far back as the 1940s. They examined the different words people used to describe functions and analysed the constructs they employed, and then synthesised this knowledge. The result was a two-dimensional map of cognitive styles that encompassed the distinctions used in the other inventories. The two dimensions are 'wholist–analytic' and 'verbaliser–imager'.

"Concept mapping works extremely well for children who are visual learners and for those who are spatially, linguistically, or logically intelligent."

Mrs. Shahida Chowdhury, Year 4 Teacher, St. Clements Church of England Primary School, Nechells, Birmingham

Below is a similar map to illustrate the dimensions of thinking inherent in the process of creating a model map. The organisation of material into the hierarchically structured branches of a model map demands an analytic perspective, while the attention paid to the overall balance and significance of the big picture is represented by the wholist end of this dimension. The use of keywords requires a verbaliser style of thinking, while the inclusion of icons draws on the mapper's skills as an imager. Model maps would seem, therefore, to reflect a balanced cognitive style.

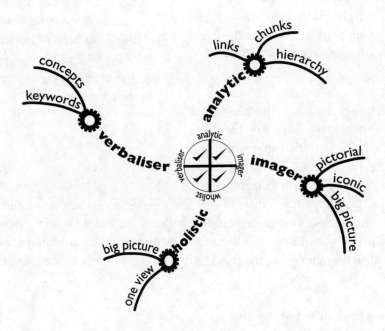

This is not how maps are usually viewed. People often dismiss maps of any sort on the assertion that they are not 'visual learners'. Put simply, because the first sense to engage a map is sight there is an assumption that they best support visual 'imager' learners and not auditory or kinaesthetic learners.

Riding and Rayner point to research that shows that non-imagers are in fact more successful in establishing stable mental images and are better at producing drawings from memory than their more 'visual' peers. There is an argument, therefore, that maps may actually be more effective for verbalisers than for imagers – the very opposite to the popular view.

"… for imagers, mental pictures are likely to be less stable than those produced by verbalisers since they will be liable to interference and displacement by further involuntary intrusive images."

Riding and Rayner (25)

In the authors' experience, it is not helpful to allocate specific activities exclusively to people appearing to fall within one of the identified categories of learners. For the student, this can lead to the construction of a belief that is not empowering. "Beliefs arise from your unwillingness to trust direct experience," asserts Smothermon (26) – in fact, Wenger claims, 80% of the brain's function is 'visual' (27), even for those with presumed auditory or kinaesthetic preferences, so we should not allow ourselves or our students to be restricted by specific labels. As Bannister suggests, "personal learning myths [about one's preferred learning style] become a handicap to effective learning" (28). Sternberg, a foremost analyst of thinking styles, reminds us that "Styles are teachable. For the most part, people acquire their styles through socialisation. But it is also possible to teach styles" (29). He suggests teachers can do this by modelling the styles themselves and explaining the advantages of each different way of thinking and learning.

This seems a perfect encouragement to teachers to learn the skills of mapping and to demonstrate its fun and effectiveness to their students. Just as Tony Buzan did, students must at some stage expect their teachers to tell them how their brain works and to suggest ways of working that are exciting and 'brain-friendly'. Mapping has enormous benefits that students will want to hear about.

◆ The bottom line

key learning skills
- create interest
- sustain concentration
- organise information
- shape memory

Students want to know how they can

- ◆ create their own interest in a subject
- ◆ sustain concentration
- ◆ organise information
- ◆ stimulate memory.

The consistent use of model mapping can significantly enhance these skills. When a map is constructed, the mapper is intensely involved in organising information. As she does this, she gets to the core of the subject, investigating how it 'clicks', and what concepts hold it together. It becomes a puzzle. Even the most uninspiring of topics can be transformed into areas of curiosity when mapping. The dullest of lengthy and bureaucratic meetings can be turned from a potentially gruelling experience into something of value – even of interest – using mapping.

When a new topic is presented too quickly, and the information cannot be linked to your existing body of knowledge, you soon lose interest because the new material has no meaning to you. Mapping allows you place it into your existing framework, starting the process of 'meaning-making'. Once this process starts, interest soon follows. You could say that mapping follows the dictum 'fake it till you make it'. Your map is your invention and as such will always offer you the possibility of fun, however little the subject or lecturer appears to be offering you.

We all find it very hard to sustain our focus – especially when faced with a blank sheet of paper and trying to formulate 'the beginning'. The trouble is that linear, sequential text has shaped our beliefs that we must always conform to that format. Learning is dependent on images and holographic thinking, but education is currently dependent on language skills and linear thinking. So teachers and students spend a great deal of effort tearing themselves away from an area of interest and forcing themselves to focus on the 'next thing' on a linear agenda, rather than making the most of the natural inclination to seek stimulation by scanning, getting an overview and experimenting in seeing new connections.

Mapping supports this natural cycle of concentration. In fact, it doesn't even feel like concentration; it feels like involvement and interest. Mapping allows, even encourages, you to follow the flow of your thoughts. It supports what could be negatively interpreted as 'flitting around'. But the interpretation depends on the intention. The mapper has the intention of understanding the topic, or of creating something new, and in this context 'flitting around' becomes an asset. Within the context of having to follow a very determined path of focus (linear text), 'flitting around' becomes negatively viewed; and that may reveal the reason why so many of our students are having problems in schools.

Some teachers bemoan the modern pop culture and its inherent lack of attention span. Forced to work within this highly visual and rapidly changing culture, it is teachers, perhaps, who could be judged to have limited concentration skills. They may be unable, or unwilling, to move from one area of focus to another so quickly, rapidly targeting attention and absorbing information from different sources. So, concentration can be defined in different ways; it depends on how you interpret it and in what context you place it.

If there is one thing we can predict with certainty, it is that we will be dealing with larger amounts of ever more complex information in the future. Model mapping gets to the heart of information management. Its very structure is dependent on analysing information and categorising content into related and hierarchically ordered branches. This process is the very essence of understanding.

With experience, you will be able to 'tame' the most daunting of collections of information, using mapping. As you become more proficient, you will be more aware of the exact questions you need to ask to understand the topic more fully. Your model map provides very real and direct feedback on how well you are organising information – if there is an item that you cannot categorise, it becomes very clear what you must find out to complete your understanding.

This awareness of being the author of the 'story' of your map, resulting from your powers of organising information, alters your relationship to learning. As described in chapter 5, the relationship of the mapper to the teacher is also radically changed.

Memory can be easily shaped and improved using memory strategies. For the most part, these relate to the short- and medium-term retention of content, and can be categorised under the term 'rote learning'. While rote learning does have a part to play in education, by far the greater part is played by 'meaningful learning', as Novak has argued so eloquently over the past 20 years (30).

> "… so-called memory tricks and other 'superlearning' strategies have little or nothing to do with meaningful learning; such promulgations are usually characterised by their avoidance of any discussion of the conceptual nature of knowledge and the strategies by which humans construct knowledge."
>
> J. D. Novak and D. B. Gowin (31)

Medium-term memory is very much supported by the use of categorisation. Back in 1969, an experiment entitled 'Hierarchical retrieval schemes in recall of categorised word lists' (32) showed just that. It showed just how effective it is to put words into groups with a common attribute. The words, however, were not necessarily meaningful. That is to say, they were not related to a subject under study. They did not form a narrative, and so give meaning. Isolated words have to be worked on, for example by connecting them to numbers, outrageous images or humorous narrative. In this way, they can be committed to medium-term memory. Some of the strategies found under the banner of accelerated learning are designed to achieve simply this, but this approach is not enough. Education should not be a content-driven, teach–test cycle, in which success can be achieved using medium-term memory tricks alone. For something to stay in a student's long-term memory, and therefore be useful in life and not just in the next exam, it must be meaningful to that student.

> "Information learned by rote (nonsense syllables and meaningless word pairs) cannot be anchored to major elements in cognitive structure and hence form a minimum linkage within it. Unless materials learned by rote are restudied repeatedly to achieve overlearning … they cannot be recalled several hours or several days after learning. Information that is learned meaningfully (associated with subsumers and cognitive structure) can usually be recalled for weeks or months after acquisition."
>
> Joseph Novak (30)

Model maps are a perfect summary of the meaning made of a subject. Additionally, as described earlier in this chapter, maps offer vital visual hooks for recall. All the aspects of recall so beloved of memory experts can be found in model maps – the strong images, the colour, the humour, the associations, the variety of size, contrast and texture – but they are placed within an organised network of meaning.

41

Mapping can produce very effective results for students preparing for and during examinations, too. The unique visual picture that every map offers is embedded in meaning in a kinaesthetic, as well as an auditory, way when the mapper 'polebridges'. Polebridging, originally developed and promoted by Wim Wenger (33), in the authors' adaptation to model mapping involves the mapper running her finger along the branches from the centre outwards. Along the line, she elaborates aloud the significance of the keyword, and at each junction explains the organising principle that led to the formation of the subsequent branches. By repeating this process for all the branches, she is 'walking her talk' manually and is creating a strong visual, auditory and kinaesthetic anchor for future recall. The potential of this technique for examinations is enormous, if the mapper is able to 'download' this stored information at the beginning, allowing herself to feel poised and relaxed before transforming the mapped knowledge to the linear text of examination writing.

◆ Use it or lose it

Armed with these skills and working from such a firm basis of confidence and enjoyment, mappers are keen to exploit the technique in as many ways as possible. They report with enthusiasm how they have used mapping to

- ◆ take notes from books, lectures, videos or computer programmes
- ◆ take notes in an interview situation or telephone conversation
- ◆ take minutes at a meeting
- ◆ make notes for essays, for revision or for a talk or presentation
- ◆ make a display
- ◆ plan a budget, a project or a shopping trip
- ◆ plan a day/week/month/term/year
- ◆ create a new idea
- ◆ solve a problem
- ◆ tell and analyse a story.

This list could be almost endless. After all, if you were to list all the applications of writing linear text, where would you stop? It is almost the same with mapping. People find mapping to be

- ◆ a faster and truer way of translating a thought onto paper than writing
- ◆ a way of supporting scanning text from a book
- ◆ a facilitative way of creating
- ◆ a way of realising how you are forming your thoughts, which some call 'helicoptering' and others call 'metacognition'
- ◆ open-ended in the way it allows for further contributions to be added
- ◆ more orderly than linear text, despite the apparent random configuration of branches

42

◆ perfectly suited for simultaneous co-operative work

◆ a way of working with many items without having to remember items listed on previous pages

◆ an easier way to handle complex ideas and issues.

You are now fully informed and ready to map. When you have learned to map (see chapter 2), and you begin to experience the benefits, you too will want to look for more areas in which to apply the technique. Remember, "Maps aren't mirrors of reality; they are a means of understanding it" (1).

Review
chapter one

CREDITS

1 Where in your life do you use physical maps?
2 Consider the possibility that for students at school going from one lesson to another without some means of fitting things together might be rather like trying to do a 2,000 piece jigsaw puzzle without the box lid.
3 Think about what you knew previously about maps and their application in schools or in your life generally. Whatnew possibilities do you see for using maps after reading this chapter?
4 Can you identify any other learning behaviours, other than the four essential learning skills outlined in this chapter, that the use of mapping would develop?

How to map

mapping demystified, deconstructed and put back together again

Chapter 2

How to map

mapping demystified, deconstructed and put back together again

COMING SOON!

1 How to select the key information needed for your maps.
2 The essential skills needed for organising information.
3 How language is organised and shapes our thinking.
4 The importance of context and purpose when producing maps.
5 Three different ways of producing your own maps.
6 The rules of model mapping.
7 How to develop your maps.
8 How it can transform making and taking notes.

How many times have you read step-by-step instructions that left you just as baffled at the end as you were before you started? The promise of learning a new skill in '10 easy lessons' lures you into the process and you keep going because you are assured that all will become clear in the end.

There are currently courses and books available to teach you how to map, but each has its own shortfalls. The procedure described in this chapter fills the gaps left by other texts, and has been used successfully by International MBA Students, teachers and students of all ages and abilities (including students with moderate learning difficulties). It will work for you too.

To help you find your way, the chapter is divided into the following sections:

◆ Unlocking texts
◆ Summary
◆ Getting it together
◆ Holographics
◆ Mapping – just like that
◆ Notes – a model mapper's perspective.

◆ Unlocking texts

This section is divided up under the following headings:

◆ Identifying keywords
◆ Context and purpose
◆ Creating meaning through keywords
◆ Keywords in everyday situations
◆ Exercises: identifying and using keywords
◆ Keywords in language hierarchies
◆ Exercises: placing words within hierarchies.

Identifying keywords

When we listen to someone speaking, or read a book, there are some words that we must pick up and understand if we are to make sense of the whole. These are keywords. The sentence 'Please get me a coffee' is completely meaningless without the keywords 'coffee' and, to a lesser degree, 'get' – the other words are not vital. It is keywords that are used in the construction of model maps.

In classrooms, keywords may well be specific to the subject being taught. They are primarily nouns, often verbs and sometimes adjectives, associated with the attitudes, skills and information under study. Unless children can identify relationships between keywords, understanding will be limited. But, of course, before they can identify relationships, they have to be able to identify the keywords themselves – this is a skill that both reflects the student's level of understanding and develops it.

Context and purpose

A road map is an incredibly compact and yet accessible way of packaging and communicating information. The context and purpose of the map will determine what information is selected to go in and how this information is organised.

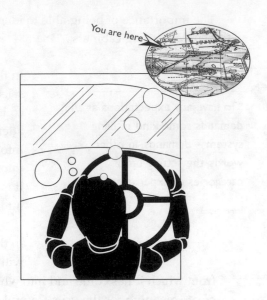
You are here

In the case of a road atlas map, much information is left out because it is outside of the *purpose* for which the map was designed; that is, to help people get from one place to another by road. For example, details of field boundaries, sites of historical interest and tourist information are not usually included on basic road maps. An Ordnance Survey map may cover the same territory but contains different information because it is designed for a different purpose.

If a road map is designed to cover the UK, the *context* of the map is the UK – it does not contain information about Europe or the rest of the world. By the same token, the map does not contain minute details of the towns or villages within the UK. Its context limits the information contained within it.

By the time you finish this book you will be able to produce maps of your school's curriculum, of the curriculum for a specific subject, of one year group within the subject, of a particular topic with that year group and even of a single lesson within the topic. You can map anything within the required context – a classroom, a school, a locality, a town, a county, a country, a global region, the world, the solar system, the universe…

Students need to see how what they are doing fits into the big picture of the lesson, the topic, the syllabus, the curriculum and their lives. The ability to identify keywords within a

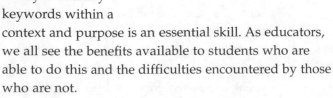

The context and purpose of the map will determine what information is selected to go in, and how this information is organised.

context and purpose is an essential skill. As educators, we all see the benefits available to students who are able to do this and the difficulties encountered by those who are not.

Creating meaning through keywords

The importance of being able to identify keywords can be illustrated by imagining two people as filing cabinets.

"To have any expectations at all demands some kind of filing system – demands, in other words, the setting up of categories of experience."

James Britton (1)

In the first filing cabinet information to be stored is selected randomly with no regard to purpose or contexts, past, present or future. In this filing cabinet no attention is paid to where this randomly selected information is placed. No understanding of the information is given and no meaning has been created. It is simply 'bunged in' along with every other piece of information that has preceded it.

In the second cabinet information is selected carefully with due consideration to the purpose and contexts from which it has come and into which it is to be placed. Keywords are identified and create meaning for the user. Careful attention is given to ensuring that the information is then stored in files that reflect the understanding and meaning created by the person. Clearly the selection and organisation of information has a direct influence on the 'user friendliness' of the filing cabinet.

Ours minds are like filing cabinets, packed with information. The only difference between us is that some of us are better at filing than others.

Keywords in everyday situations

Identifying and using keywords is one of the first things we learn to do as children and it is something we still do quite naturally at times for various reasons. It is not necessarily a skill that we consciously use as a means to help us organise information

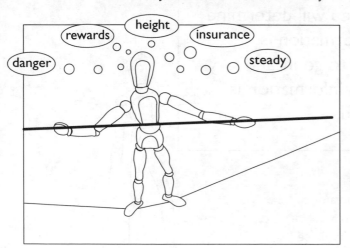

and learn meaningfully, but if you can make this very natural process more obvious and evident you will be better equipped to start mapping.

When children learn to speak there is a stage when single words develop from sounds to communicate a need or emotion. We don't have to be wizards to fill in a sentence around single words spoken by a toddler: "mum … juice … please". Even as adults, we often find ourselves in excited or stressful states that render us unable to speak in full sentences and yet still able to convey the meaning! The words that come out are the keywords – words that best convey the whole message we want to put across.

When we try to recollect an event from memory we often find ourselves searching for a particular word – we might say it's 'on the tip of the tongue'. Often it is the name of a person or place that we are searching for. Once we recollect the word, a whole series of thoughts and emotions come back to us associated with the circumstances and sensations we experienced at the time. The keyword 'unlocks' all these connected thoughts.

We all use keywords in an entirely natural way. Words are selected to convey a meaning either to ourselves or to others. Information associated with the keyword is stored 'with it', and can be recollected along with it at a future date. The word 'recollect' literally means 'to call back to mind'; that is to say, the word has already been collected and stored some time before. The exercises that follow are designed to demonstrate and develop your ability to select keywords for your maps.

Exercises: identifying and using keywords

Exercise 1

You will need a piece of paper and a pen or pencil for this exercise.

Think back to a holiday or a day out that you really enjoyed. Remember as much detail as possible about your visit and write as much as you can. You could write about the location, the weather, people, travel arrangements, food, feelings, thoughts, funniest/scariest/best/worst moments, or anything else that you can recall. Keep going until it would be impossible to fit all of your writing onto a postcard, even if you were able to type the information, reduce it in size and then stick it on! Now put your piece of paper to the back of the book and read on – we will return to your trip after the next exercise.

Exercise 2

Below is an extract from a book, in which the nouns, verbs and adjectives have been left out. Try to guess what the extract is about.

_____, the _____ _____ of a _____ _____ a lot of _____ from the _____ on the _____ and _____. Perhaps our _____ _____ towards _____ _____ in our _____ through _____ _____ and _____ _____ is _____. In _____ for the _____ and _____ of _____ _____ we _____ _____ for the _____ of the _____ and _____ _____ that _____ _____ of our _____ _____. We are all _____.

It's difficult to make any sense of it with so much missing. Now try this version, with only the nouns and verbs missing.

> _____, the school _____ of a _____ _____ a lot of _____ from the _____ on the _____ and _____. Perhaps our natural _____ towards _____ _____ in our _____ through visual _____ and spatial _____ is undervalued. In _____ for the _____ and _____ of _____ _____ we are _____ for the _____ of the visual and spatial _____ that _____ _____ of our neural _____. We are all _____.

Still, it is very hard to create any accurate meaning from the extract. Try it with only nouns missing.

> _____, the school _____ of a _____ places a lot of _____ from the _____ on the _____ and _____. Perhaps our natural _____ towards organising _____ in our _____ through visual _____ and spatial _____ is undervalued. In arguing for the _____ and _____ of _____ _____ we are arguing for the _____ of the visual and spatial _____ that seems _____ of our neural _____. We are all _____.

Even now, the meaning is far from clear. The point is that nouns carry more meanings and associations than any other words. Verbs also help us to understand and make meaning, as do adjectives, though to a lesser extent. But the words that help make most sense of the extract are nouns. Here is the full text to illustrate the point.

> Nowadays, the school experience of a child places a lot of emphasis from the outset on the written and spoken. Perhaps our natural disposition towards organising information in our heads through visual patterns and spatial relationships is undervalued. In arguing for the teaching and use of mapping techniques we are arguing for the extension of the visual and spatial propensity that seems part of our neural architecture. We are all mappers (2).

Exercise 3 [exercise 1 revisited]

Now go back to exercise 1. Highlight all the nouns, verbs and adjectives in the piece of writing about your trip. If you were to write these words alone on a postcard, how much information about your trip would the recipient be able to glean from it

1 if the words were not organised in any particular way

2 if the words were arranged as in the examples shown.

These postcards were sent by year 12 students during the summer vacation that followed their introduction to mapping.

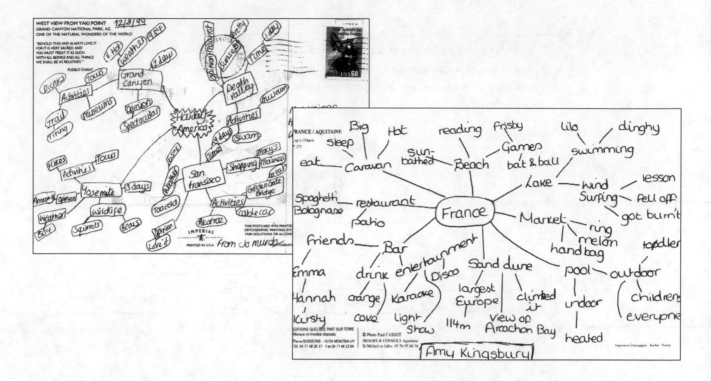

Keywords in language hierarchies

Having an understanding of the hierarchical relationships between word meanings will help you select and use keywords in your maps. It will also mean that you (and your students) will be able to discern relationships between concepts represented through language (keywords) on your maps. In so doing you will be learning meaningfully.

"It is the hierarchical relationships between word meanings that has most evidently far reaching influence upon our thinking. Anyone who has played guessing games where the answer is restricted to [two choices] will recognise the strategy that follows the hierarchical relationships somewhat after this fashion."

James Britton (1)

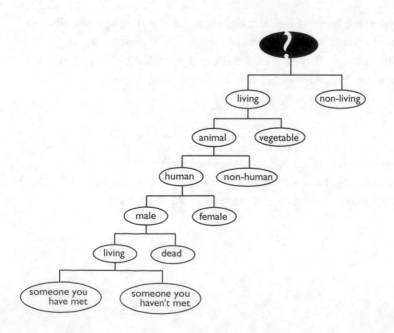

"... [hierarchies] lie behind most of our ordinary use of language. As we arrive at a decision in a matter of colour – say, in talk with a friend – we may use words at descending levels of such a classification ..."

James Britton (I)

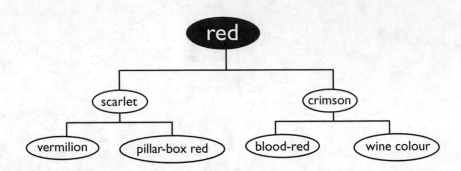

A map of a classroom could be viewed as a 'sub-map' of a map of the school, which in turn is contained within a map of the locality. The locality is within the town, the town within the county, the county within the country, and so on. Concepts represented

"The form of a classification must depend in fact upon its purpose. For the purpose of buying and selling, for example, a shop might divide clothes into 'ready made' and 'made to measure', but this distinction would have no relevance for a man who was organising his holiday packing ..."

James Britton (I)

through language follow the same hierarchical arrangement. Model maps physically portray the relationships of language within a particular context. In chapter 4, we examine how to teach the thinking skills associated with and revealed by model maps; a key element of this process is teaching students how language is organised.

"The hierarchical organisation is, of course, dependent on the context we are dealing with, and a remarkable characteristic of our minds is that we may use the same concepts in many different contexts and many different hierarchies."

Joseph Novak (3)

Visually, we can represent this hierarchical ordering of language as a triangle. The diagram shown is an example of this.

Towards the bottom of the triangle hierarchy we have some common names of some specific flowers – 'buttercup', 'bluebell' and 'daisy'. If we think of 'buttercup', we may think of the words 'yellow', 'shiny' and 'pretty'. These words come to mind *after* thinking of 'buttercup'. When we think of 'wild flowers', we do not think of 'yellow', 'shiny' and 'pretty' until after we have thought of the names of wild flowers, specifically 'buttercup'. Above 'wild flowers' on the hierarchy, we have 'flowers', and above this 'plants'; if we think of the word 'plants' we are even less likely to think 'yellow', 'shiny' and 'pretty'.

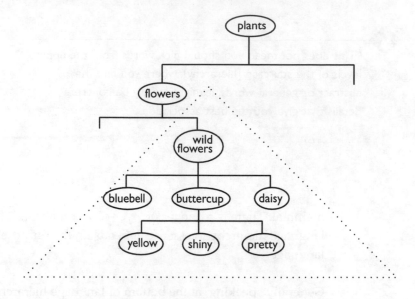

So, we only think of the descriptive words related to the buttercup after we have thought of the buttercup. Notice that the higher up the language triangle we travel, the more abstract or general the terminology becomes.

All words can be organised into hierarchies. The diagram below illustrates this beautifully.

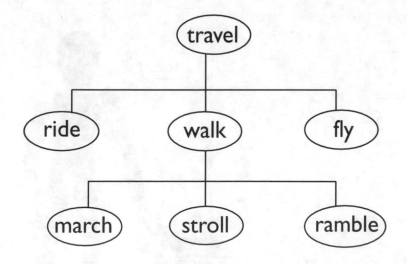

Harry Alder and Beryl Heather (4)

The conceptual level of the language we use has to be sufficiently high to be able to group together all the 'things', 'ideas', and 'actions' of the concept being examined. However, If we go too high up the hierarchy we may lose many of the associations that occur at the level we're interested in. For example, if we were to ask a student to write a story about her pet, Rover, it would be useful for the student to tell us that Rover is a dog and that he is one of several furry domestic pets at home. For the purpose of the story, however, it is not necessary for the student to tell us that Rover is a mammal. There is a danger of 'over-conceptualising'. The level at which we enter the language hierarchy in essence depends on the purpose for which we are using the language.

> "This does not mean you should pick words from the upper levels of the staircase [hierarchy], where you find the abstract or general words. It might equally be concrete details that give you the best associations."
>
> *I. Svantesson (5)*

Generally speaking, at the bottom of language hierarchies we tend to have specific details of language. As we move towards the top of the hierarchy we move towards less specific and more general words that can overlap or encompass the words below. In effect, we move from a concrete level of detailed language at the bottom to an abstract level at the top.

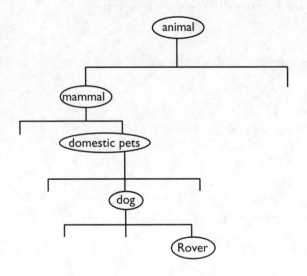

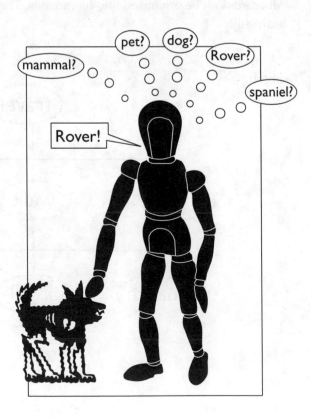

Another example of hierarchical levels of language is shown in the diagram below.

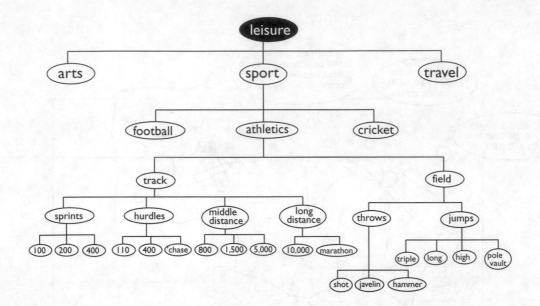

Terms like 'javelin', '100 metres', 'long jump', and 'pole vault' may release in our minds words associated with these events. The words 'track' and 'field' could release not only the events given above (javelin etc.) but also other associated events – these words are at a higher level on our language triangle, and so have more terms subordinate to them.

As we proceed further up the triangle, so we reach a greater level of abstraction. You cannot *see* 'athletics' – you can only see examples of athletics events. Similarly, you cannot *see* 'track events' or 'field events' – you can only see examples of them. If you were asked to plan a talk about 'athletics' you would not include football or cricket (although, of course, players of these sports are athletes of their own discipline). If, however, you were asked to plan a talk about 'sport' you could include athletics, football and cricket within your selection. The level at which you enter the hierarchy depends upon your purpose.

When you create a model map, you are setting down the language hierarchy associated with the concept under examination. The part of the hierarchy you use in your map depends upon your purpose – in the example above, you may wish to examine the details of track events in athletics, or you may want to create a general overview of popular leisure activities. The associations you make within your map may well be different from those in the example, but the key is to ensure that they are arranged hierarchically – each new word should be 'contained' within the concept word to which you attach it (as 'track' is contained within 'athletics', and 'pole vault' is contained within 'jumps').

"When we classify in accordance with the words that name objects ... we are creating categories that are [1] on the same lines as those other people have made and [2] in accordance with describable general criteria."

James Britton (1)

When mapping, it is important to imagine language triangles the whole time you are working with your subject area or context. Ask yourself questions such as:

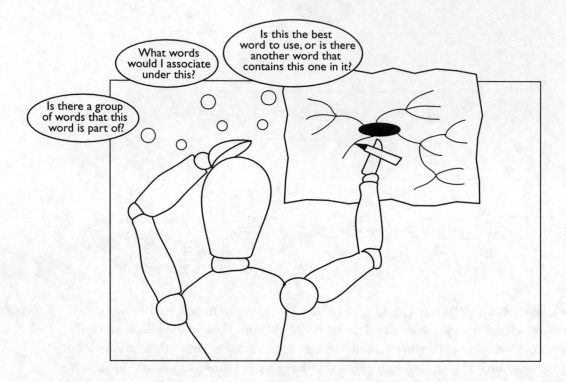

With practice, you will become adept at choosing the word that best releases all the associated ideas beneath.

It is tempting when you start mapping to think that you need to use lots of keywords in order to record, and therefore remember, information – you don't. The exercises below are designed to help you see how best to select keywords by 'seeing' and using language triangles.

Exercises: placing words into language hierarchies

Exercise 1

What words could you use to describe or group the following collections of words?

1 table, chair, bed, sofa

2 tennis, badminton, squash

3 bee, wasp, ant, fly

Exercise 2

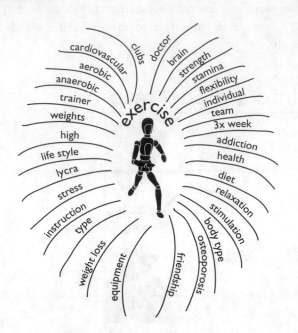

You will need three or four sheets of paper to do this exercise. Draw a small circle in the middle of a page, with lines radiating out from it. Write the word 'exercise' in the circle. Follow the model given above to 'brainstorm' words you associate with 'exercise', and write them on the radiating lines. It does not matter if your words are not the same as those in the example.

Next, on another sheet of paper, group together words that you associate with one another. In the top right diagram, for example, the words 'individual', 'team' and 'weights' are grouped together.

Now try to identify the keyword that would link all the words in each group together. If you cannot identify a word that links or associates them all together check to see if they do, in fact, go together. Sometimes you will need to move words to another group or start another category altogether. In the example, the word 'type' is used to group together the words 'team', 'individual' and 'weights' – they all different types of exercise. Can you think of any other types of exercise that you could add?

Now think back to the language hierarchies we were looking at earlier. What information could you add at the bottom of this 'triangle'? In other words, what examples of 'team', 'individual' or 'weights' exercises could you add?

As you can see, the keywords used to organise the information on exercise in the example are written near the centre of the map, and are not necessarily contained within the original brainstorm. We have to go 'higher' up the language hierarchy to find words to organise the information most effectively.

fitting language triangles into a model map

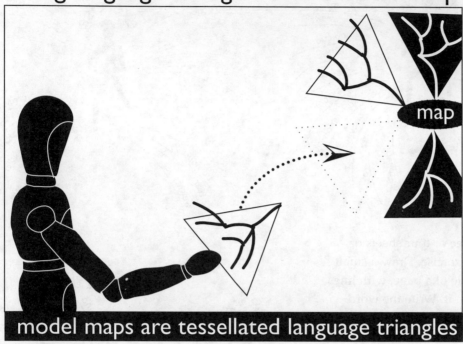

model maps are tessellated language triangles

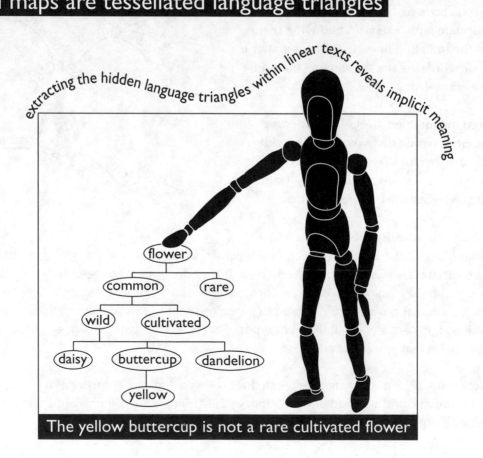

extracting the hidden language triangles within linear texts reveals implicit meaning

The yellow buttercup is not a rare cultivated flower

MAPWISE — accelerated learning through visible thinking

◆ Summary

In this chapter so far we have:

- ◆ seen how we can identify keywords in language
- ◆ seen how language can be organised into hierarchies or 'triangles'
- ◆ seen that the number and types of words that can be associated with a keyword depend upon the level in the hierarchy from which you choose the keyword
- ◆ practised identifying keywords
- ◆ introduced the idea that language hierarchies are, in effect, ways of categorising information.

The next section examines and teaches you how to classify and categorise information, which is the essential thinking skill of mapping. If you had difficulty with the exercises in the previous section, the exercises that follow are designed to support you in identifying hierarchical relationships.

◆ Getting it together

This section is divided up under the following headings:

- ◆ Classification and categorisation – cornerstones for meaningful learning
- ◆ Organising principles around us
- ◆ Exercises

Classification and categorisation — cornerstones for meaningful learning

From the moment we are born, we are trying to make sense of the world around us. As we grow and develop, new experiences start to take on two distinct forms: they seem to us to be either *similar* to previous experiences or *different* from them. It is only in *comparing* that we can see a similarity or a difference. If we did not do this our ability to understand what is happening around us would be limited; our ability to create meaning in the world would be curtailed.

It is not too great a generalisation to state that children and adults with learning disabilities have difficulty organising and making sense of information. We could say that they have difficulties in learning meaningfully; that is, they have difficulty in identifying and

"It is only through spontaneously making comparisons that children (or adults) can be modified by the arrival of new stimuli. They have to organise new experiences according to how they can relate them to, and compare them with, what they already know and think. Relationships are established through comparison."

Mike Lake, Author of Top Ten Thinking Tactics (6)

61

explaining relationships between concepts. These concepts could be objects or events (or both). Until a relationship or meaning is established, learning is episodic.

In order to promote meaningful learning in schools, educators must have an understanding of how meaning itself is created. It is very clear from a student's work whether he has *understood* what has been taught or has simply learned what has been taught without creating any meaning for himself. Meaningful learning does happen in schools now, but it happens almost by accident. Until we understand *how* meaningful learning takes place we cannot *ensure* that it does so. Chapter 7 examines in detail how meaning is created.

What if we were able to reveal exactly how we create meaning? It is the skill of making comparisons, of identifying similarities and differences, that enables us to form concepts and identify relationships between these concepts. This is a fundamental skill, the full significance of which has seemingly not yet been grasped by the educational world. To learn meaningfully – to make sense of the world around us – we need either to establish how information presented to us is organised or to create a way of organising it for ourselves. We need to categorise our experiences. Most of the time we do this automatically. When we cannot do so, we can feel anxious. When we do succeed, we may fall into the trap of thinking that our way of organising things is the only 'right' way.

In his book, *Mind Power* (7), Edward De Bono sets out an exercise where the reader is asked to work out different ways in which eight different items can be connected by common concepts. The items he uses are:

boat	**tree**	**ant**	**duck**
pig	**tap**	**clock**	**cloud**

This exercise demonstrates how we can get stuck with an initial viewpoint and not see alternatives. It also shows that the same information can form different groups depending on the organising concept. For example, 'boat', 'tap' and 'clock' can be linked together under the organising principle of 'manufactured by humans' – the others all occur naturally. 'Tree', 'ant', 'pig' and 'duck' could be linked together under the organising principle of 'living organisms'. What items would you place under the following organising principles?

 linked to water

 large

 found in a house.

Organising principles around us

Retailers use organising principles to lay out their goods on the shop floor, to help customers find what they need easily. In this case, the 'information' they are organising is not text or words but goods. Try to imagine the shop as a map with each of the sections labelled according to its contents.

There are many different organising principles that shops can use, but we can only shop effectively once we have worked out how things have been organised. Having visited a shop a few times, we form a mental map of the layout. As soon as the shop undergoes a refit or reorganisation, our mental map becomes useless and we are left feeling confused, until we can work out the new organisation.

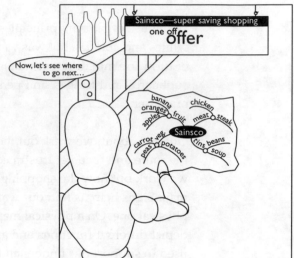

One particular arrangement is not necessarily any better than another, but to establish an organising principle is extremely useful in helping to make sense of information. Think how confusing it would be to visit a supermarket to find no organisational layout to the goods at all. The organising principle that is chosen depends, to a large extent, on its purpose. For example, in a DIY shop paints might be organised according to type, as in arrangement A below. In a brochure designed to help customers plan their home decorating, however, the paints available might be organised according to colour and shade (as in B below).

A

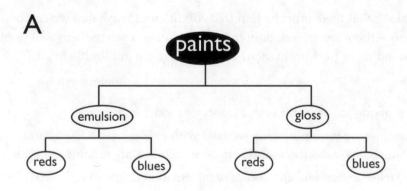

B

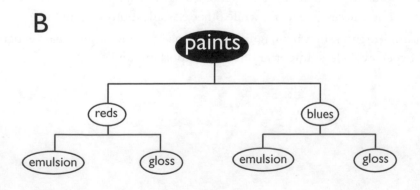

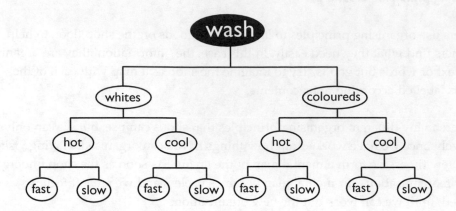

We all use organising principles all the time. At home, we may organise washing into whites and colours, hot wash and cool wash, fast spin and slow spin. We organise types of furniture into different rooms, clothes into wardrobes, money into accounts, food into cupboards and fridges, and personal lives and details into cabinets, PCs and personal organisers.

Out and about, we work out the best route to get somewhere, we form a mental map of the route and then get frustrated if we are forced to leave the intended route. On arrival, we work out how the shopping centre or event or location is organised by locating a map. Signs help us find our way around the map whether it be a mental one or a physical one. On a physical map, different fonts, type sizes or colours may be used to depict different functions and areas. Being aware of the way organising principles are used to support our understanding will help you when you start to map.

You may be thinking that there must be hundreds of different ways that we can organise information. Relax – there are, in fact, only five ways (8), and each of them will permit a different understanding of the information. The following are applicable to any endeavour.

- ◆ **Category** – goods are organised by category or model in a shop
- ◆ **Time** – used for organising items associated with events over a fixed duration; for example, museums, exhibitions and historical accounts are organised in this way
- ◆ **Location** – used to examine and compare information originating from different sources
- ◆ **Alphabet** – often used to organise large bodies of information; since we all know the alphabet, it is accessible to all, while other classifications may not be
- ◆ **Continuum** – organisation by magnitude, such as 'small to large', 'least expensive to most expensive', 'least important to most important' and so on.

"Uncovering the organising principles is like having the ultimate hatrack. It is essential when working with already existing bodies of information, as it is in developing your own information. The time spent comprehending someone else's method of organisation will reduce the search time spent looking for individual components."

Richard Saul Wurman (8)

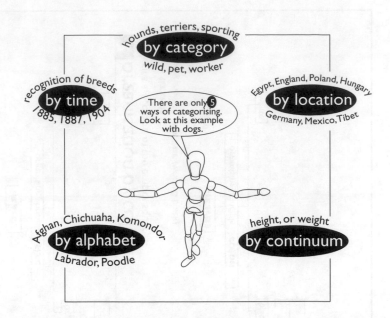

Exercises

The following exercises, shown on pages 66–68, are designed to help you organise information when mapping. (Note that these exercises are available in photocopiable A4 format as a separate workbook – please see page 2 for details.)

Organisation of Lizards

On page 66, on sheets 1 and 2, are four lizards, labelled a, b, c, d. They represent units of information that need organising. Do parts 1 and 2 of the exercise to indicate how they could be organised, first according to size and second by colour. The third chart shows how they could be organised by size and colour.

Organisation of monsters

On page 67, on sheets 3 and 4, are four monsters labelled a, b, c, d. Follow the instructions given below the monsters and complete parts 1, 2, 3 and 4.

Organisation of geometric shapes

The series of exercises shown on page 68, on sheets 5 and 6, uses geometric shapes as an analogy for written information. There are a number of different shapes of different sizes and colours. At present they are not organised or classified in any way. Part 1 of this exercise asks you to collect your data. Part 2 asks you to establish the possible principles of classification that you could use to organise the shapes. Part 3 asks you to classify the shapes according to shape, colour and size.

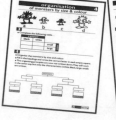

65

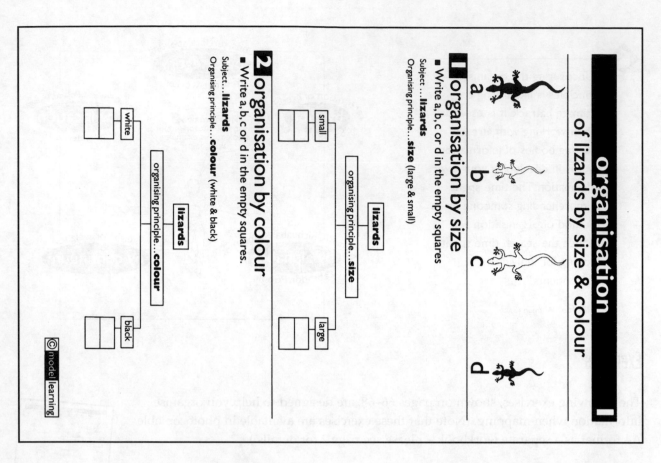

organisation
of lizards by size & colour

1

a ▬ b ▬ c ▬ d ▬

1 organisation by size

■ Write a, b, c or d in the empty squares

Subject…**lizards**
Organising principle…**size** (large & small)

small — lizards — large

organising principle…**size**

2 organisation by colour

■ Write a, b, c or d in the empty squares.

Subject…**lizards**
Organising principle…**colour** (white & black)

white — lizards — black

organising principle…**colour**

© model learning

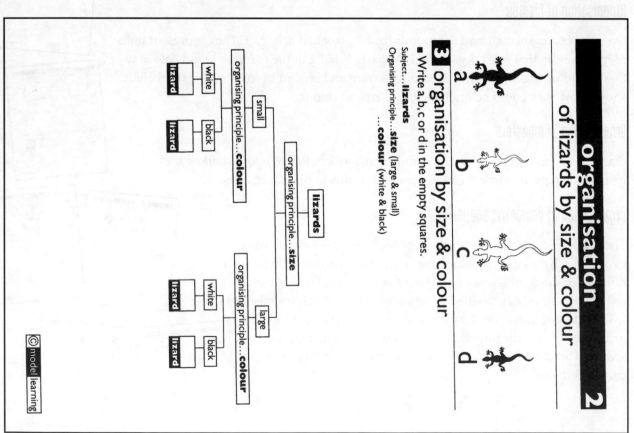

organisation
of lizards by size & colour

2

a ▬ b ▬ c ▬ d ▬

3 organisation by size & colour

■ Write a, b, c or d in the empty squares.

Subject…**lizards**
Organising principle…**size** (large & small)
…**colour** (white & black)

lizards

organising principle…**size**

small — organising principle…**colour**
  white — lizard
  black — lizard

large — organising principle…**colour**
  white — lizard
  black — lizard

© model learning

4 organisation
of monsters by size & colour

a   b   c   d

3
- Complete the following table...

colour		size
black	white	small
		large

4
- Organise the monsters by size and colour.
- Fill in the headings and write the correct letter in each empty square.
- The organising principles are now not written down. They still work in the same way but only the characteristics (white, black, large, small) are written.

monsters

monster   monster   monster   monster

---

3 organisation
of monsters by size & colour

a   b   c   d

1
- Fill in what is missing...
- White monsters... ☐ and ☐
- Black monsters... ☐ and ☐
- Large monsters... ☐ and ☐
- Small monsters... ☐ and ☐

- Monster **a** is... **black and large**
- Monster **b** is...............................
- Monster **c** is...............................
- Monster **d** is...............................

2
- Which monster is small and white?... ☐
- Which monster is black and large?... ☐
- What do monsters **b** and **d** have in common?.................
- What do monsters **a** and **d** have in common?.................
- Which pairs of monsters are dissimilar both in colour and size?...
  pair ☐ and ☐ ... and pair ☐ and ☐

organisation
of geometric shapes
5

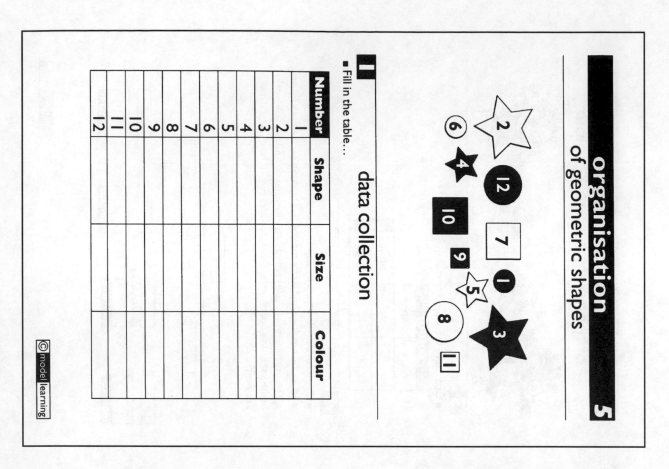

1 Fill in the table…

data collection

Number	Shape	Size	Colour
1			
2			
3			
4			
5			
6			
7			
8			
9			
10			
11			
12			

organisation
of geometric shapes
6

establishing organising principles
2

- How many different **shapes** have you found?…… ☐
- What are they?……………………………
- How many different **sizes** have you found?… ☐
- What are they?……………………………
- How many different **colours** have you found?… ☐
- What are they?……………………………

organisation according to shape, size and colour
3

- Organise the twelve geometric shapes according to shape, size and colour
- Write the numbers of the shapes in the correct places in this organisation chart

geometric shapes

organisation principle…**shape**

Number
Number
Number
Number
Number
Number
Number
Number
Number
Number
Number
Number

9 mapping classification
of pets

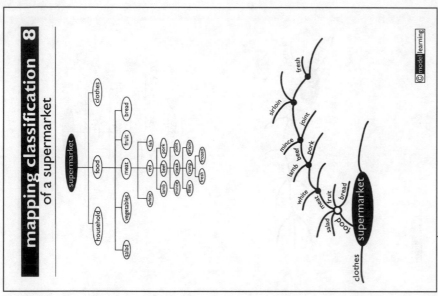

8 mapping classification
of a supermarket

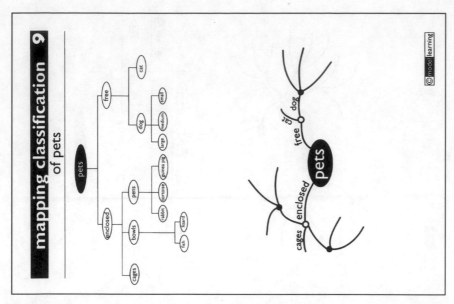

7 mapping classification
of a shoe shop

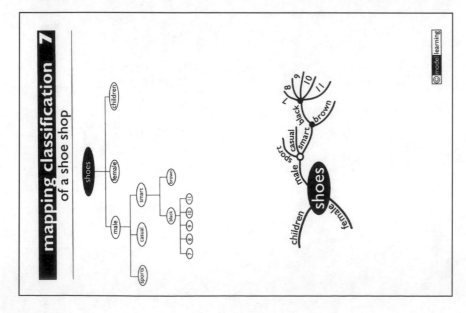

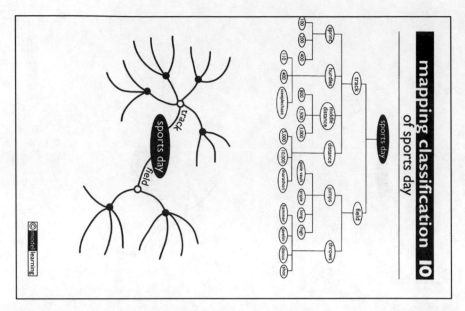

mapping classification 10
of sports day

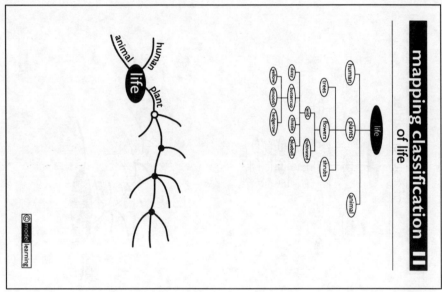

mapping classification 11
of life

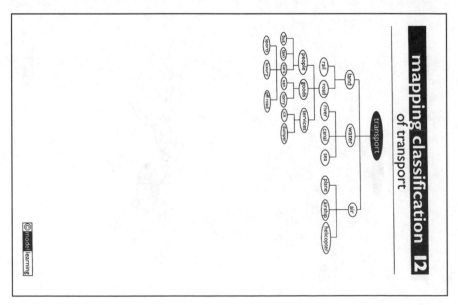

mapping classification 12
of transport

◆ Holographics

In this section you will find cloze procedure exercises designed to take you from linear to holographic thinking, and thereby help you use your classification skills in the production of maps.

Exercises

(Note that these exercises are available in photocopiable A4 format as a separate workbook – please see page 2 for details.)

Look at the first mapping classification diagram on page 69, sheet 7. At the top is shown one possible classification tree for a shoe shop. The main classification of the stock is by intended wearer – the shoes are divided up under 'male', 'female' and 'children'. Beneath the classification 'male' the shoes are classified into 'types'; namely 'sports', 'casual', and 'smart'. (The same classification could have been used for 'female' and 'children', but for the purpose of the exercise only the 'male' shoes have been classified.) The classification tree goes on to show the organisation of the shoes according to colour and size.

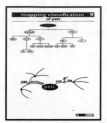

Below the tree is a model map of the same information. The subject of the classification, 'shoes', is at the centre and the main organising or classification principles – namely 'male', 'female' and 'children' – radiate from the centre. The organising principles of male shoes – 'sports', 'casual' and 'smart' – then branch off from 'male'. Note that there is room to classify the 'female' and 'children' shoes in the same way here if required, whereas there was little space in the classification tree. The same information is represented in a different way.

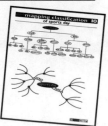

Ultimately this is what a model map is: a series of key ideas or principles stemming from, and classified around, a central theme or idea.

On pages 69 and 70, sheets 8 to 12, other information has been classified and then represented in a model map, in the same way as for the shoe shop. Go through these in order. Copy out each model map onto a blank sheet of paper. You will see that more and more information has been omitted in each subsequent exercise. Your job is to fill in the gaps.

The purpose of these exercises is twofold. First, it is to help you see that model maps are effectively a series of classifications around a central point. Second, it provides you with the opportunity to start writing and representing information in a new way.
Work through the exercises now. As you go though ask yourself these questions:

◆ In what other ways could this information have been organised?

◆ Where else in my life do I already organise information like this?

◆ Mapping — just like that

This section is divided up under the following headings:

- ◆ How to produce a map – a step-by-step guide
- ◆ Key rules to follow when mapping
- ◆ Step-by-step guide to mapping, version 1 – dump it, organise it, map it (DOM)
- ◆ Step-by-step guide to mapping, version 2 – the book analogy
- ◆ Step-by-step guide to mapping, version 3 – the literal approach
- ◆ Ways to develop your maps

How to produce a map — a step-by-step guide

The map on page 77 is about the benefits of mapping. This section takes you through the thinking that took place to produce this map – it *models* the authors' thinking. Where keywords used on the map appear here in the text, they are in bold type, to model the selection and use of keywords within a map.

1   We started by asking ourselves these questions:

- ◆ What is the purpose of the map?
- ◆ In what context is it to be used?

The context for the map was an educational leaflet to be distributed to schools. Its purpose was to illustrate the benefits of mapping in a way that was readily understandable (without additional explanation) to its audience – the teaching profession.

2   Being clear about the purpose from the start helped us to decide later which information to put in and which to leave out. It also meant we were able to come up with a title for our map that would itself be the main organising principle. The title – Benefits – came to us during the discussion since all the ideas we wanted to communicate came under this heading. We placed the word '**benefits**' at the centre of the page.

3   We then had to decide what the main organising principles would be for our map – we had to establish what the main branches from the centre would contain. We quickly decided that we wanted to focus on **teaching** and **learning** and so we added these branches to our map.

4   We then discussed what information we wanted to contain within these headings. We discussed how learning involves committing things to memory and in turn how long-term memory depends on actually **understanding** the concepts or information being learned. We also discussed how mapping supports the learner in creating interest, sustaining concentration, organising information and shaping **memory**. The acquisition of these **skills** promotes certain qualities or attitudes in learners; it can make learners more resilient, resourceful and responsible for their work.

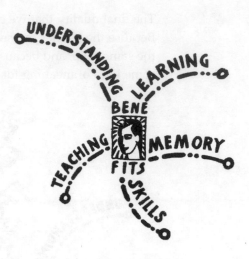

Each of these three keywords – 'understanding', 'memory' and 'skills' – needed further elaboration so at this point we faced a choice. We could either use them as sub-headings branching off from 'learning', or we could emphasise their importance by giving them their own branches. As you can see, we decided on the latter. We now had five main branches.

5   We then moved randomly around the branches adding sub-heading as we discussed them. Because this account is written in linear form it is hard to recreate the random nature of our discussion but if we take each of the branches in turn we can walk you through our thinking.

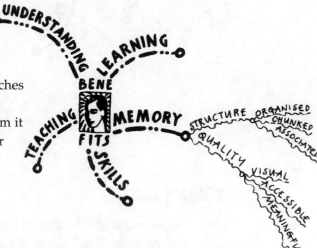

The 'memory' branch

6   We decided that the two main reasons why mapping supports long-term memory are its **qualities** and its **structure**. We discussed having the structure of the map as one of the qualities – that is, having 'structure' branching off from 'qualities' – but because we wanted to emphasise the importance of structure, we gave it a separate branch off from 'memory'.

7   A map's structure is **organised** hierarchically so that the learner can see which information is contained within each section. It is **chunked** so that the learner can see which elements go together. This also helps the learner to see relationships within the whole. The fact that the whole is always visible supports the learner in making **associations** with other areas of the map.

8   We decided to emphasise three qualities of maps. First, research shows that our capacity for **visual** recall is vast. As each map, unlike linear text, is visually unique, so it helps us to remember. A map's layout means that, unlike linear text, the information is always **accessible** and it is easy to add or show relationships.

73

The final quality that we chose to emphasise was the **meaningful** nature of maps. Because the learner can see relationships between the parts and the whole all at the same time, and because she has had to organise the information, she creates some kind of meaning for herself.

The 'learning' branch

9　Because we made the earlier decision of creating separate branches for 'memory', 'understanding' and 'skills', we discussed what other benefits we could highlight for 'learners'. We decided to map the **qualities** that mapping promotes in learners and to emphasise that model mapping is a very effective method for making and taking **notes**.

10　Our experience of working with students in schools is that once learners know how they learn they become more **resilient** – it's as if they 'know that they can know' so they are less likely to 'give up'. Learners with mapping skills are therefore far more **resourceful** and able to take more **responsibility** for forging meaning and understanding for themselves. (Along with 'resilience', these qualities make up the 'three Rs'.)

11　Using mapping to take notes while listening to a speaker supports the learner, and helps to make the experience less like dictation followed by handwriting exercise. The notes become **full** as the learner is supported in seeing and making connections. Because keywords or concepts are identified, the process is **fast**.

Because thinking is visually supported the act becomes more **fun**. The demand for structure that is inherent in mapping makes note-making more purposeful. The learner can see how their notes are hierarchical in nature. They are supported in making their thinking clear.

The 'skills' branch

12 As a learner learns he displays certain skills. During the learning process, the learner must be **interested**, able to **concentrate**, **organise information** and **memorise** the work. This entire section is very closely associated with the rest of the map: there is a whole branch on 'memory', 'organising information' is directly linked to the 'understanding' branch and 'interest' and 'concentration' are a direct consequence of the 'three Rs' found in the 'learning' branch. Mapping contributes directly to the development of these skills.

The 'teaching' branch

13 We discussed how we could show succinctly that model mapping has impact in all areas of a teacher's work. We decided to use the '**plan–do–review**' model since we felt teachers would recognise this without further explanation.

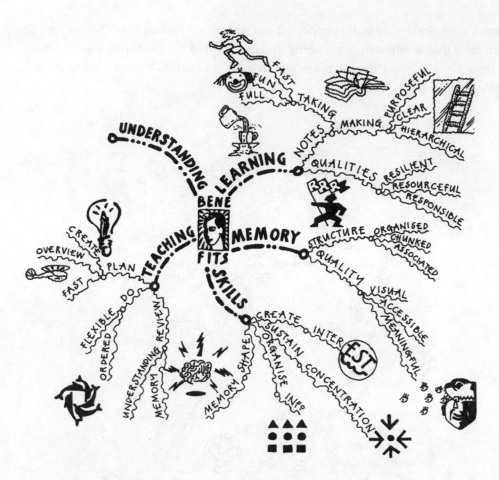

14 Using mapping to plan work, meetings or presentations is **fast**. You have an **overview** available to you at any time and, as explained in chapter 7, it is a great way to make planning a more **creative** experience.

In chapters 6 and 7 you will see the impact that mapping can have on **flexible** and **ordered** classroom delivery. You will also find out how mapping can be used to gauge students' **understanding** of your delivery and why it is such a powerful **memory** technique.

The 'understanding' branch

15 We believe that teaching and learning is all about helping the learner to understand. We wanted to emphasise this, so we gave understanding a branch of its own. We then discussed how a model map promoted understanding and we decided to map the three main ways.

Without a map, learning is like trying to do a jigsaw puzzle without the lid of the box. Learners need to see how the individual pieces fit into the whole – the **big picture**. It is also clear that you cannot understand something unless you **organise the information** in some way such that it makes sense to you. Using maps in this way also enables you to see **connections** between different areas of the map. As the full map on the opposite page shows, there are many connections to be made between the individual elements.

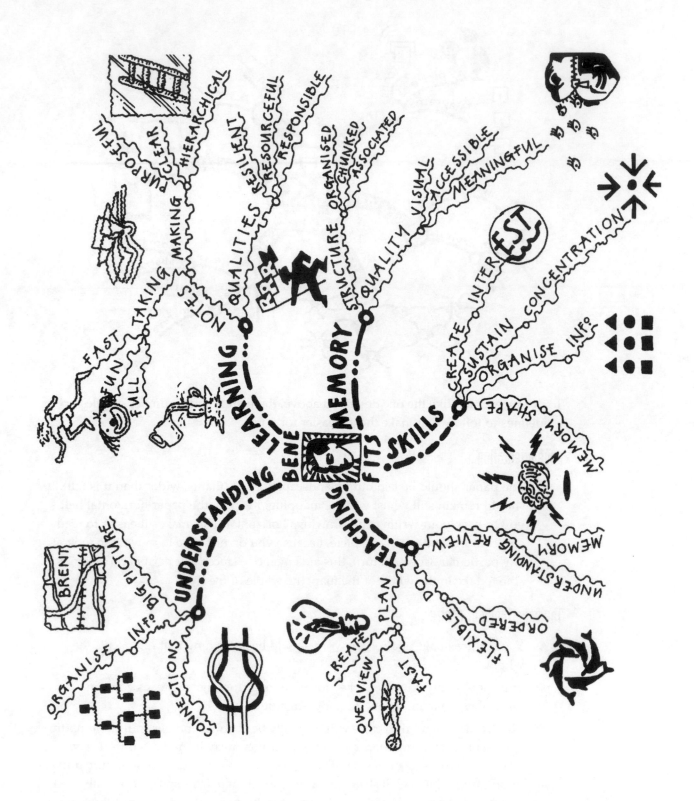

Key rules to follow when mapping

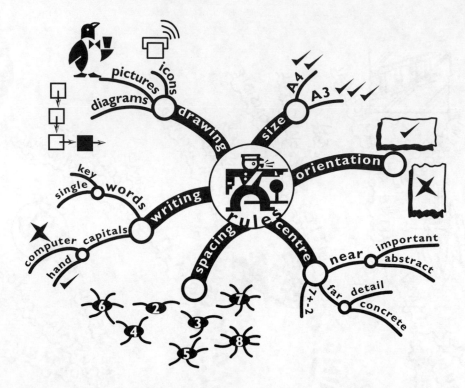

To produce a map like the one described above, there are a small number of rules or guidelines to follow that make the job easier for you.

Page orientation

◆ The paper should be laid out in landscape format (that is, wider than it is tall). It should remain still whilst you are mapping. Keeping the paper horizontal helps you to keep your writing and drawings horizontal. This makes it easier to read and comprehend when complete, because you do not have to move it to look at any particular aspect. In turn, this aids memory, since your peripheral vision is able to take in the whole of the map, the whole of the time.

The importance of centre

◆ Your centre image and/or keyword should be something that represents the whole.

◆ You should only have 7 (±2) key ideas coming from the centre, as you can remember a maximum of 7 (±2) ideas readily.

◆ The words around the centre will normally be abstract and generalised in nature and be of greater importance than those further away from the centre. The words towards the outside of the map will be more concrete or specific in nature but less important to the overall structure of the model map. Having 7 (±2) key abstract words at the centre provides a platform for the rest of the map to build upon, since they, if chosen correctly, will have a large potential to 'capture' subordinate ideas.

Spacing

◆ The number of branches you have coming from the centre will affect the use of space on the paper. After mapping for a while you develop an ability to predict the space you will need for each branch.

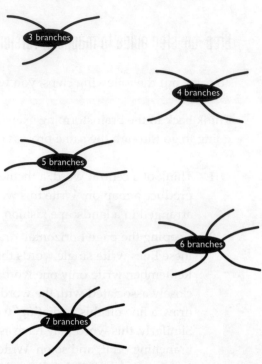

◆ The branches should be spread evenly around the centre and the branches kept as horizontal as possible at all times. The areas to the left and right of centre are easiest to map on; the areas above and below centre are the hardest. Look at the maps at the start of each chapter, and the diagrams to the right which model ideal spacing.

◆ White space is important as it provides borders for the words and images on your map. It helps them to stand out and therefore helps you to remember them. It also represents the space in which additional ideas, and explanations of the relationships between the key concepts, can – and do – show up.

Writing

◆ Use single words wherever possible. This makes additional associations easier.

◆ As we saw earlier, nouns carry most meanings and associations. Use them as much as possible rather than verbs, adjectives and so on.

◆ Use capital letters: they are easier to read, tend to be neater and are therefore easier to commit to memory (unless of course your small case writing is particularly neat, in which case use whatever you feel most comfortable with).

◆ You can give words at the centre added emphasis by making them bolder and bigger than those towards the periphery.

Using icons, pictures and graphic images

◆ Icons, pictures and graphic images can be used to replace many words and/or to summarise whole sections of a map. Just as a noun will stimulate more associations in your memory than a verb, so an image can stimulate a whole series of thoughts and memories. When we think of a noun we automatically see an image of it in our mind's eye, but when we see a picture or image it stimulates more of our senses than a single word.

Size of paper

◆ You can map onto any size of paper. The authors send post cards that are mapped! A3 is a good size as it allows plenty of space, but A4 may be more convenient for storing.

Step-by-step guide to mapping, version 1 — dump it, organise it, map it (DOM)

To carry out the following steps, you will need three or four sheets of blank paper.

Think back to the brainstorming exercise on the word 'exercise' (page 59). You are now going to go through the same process on a subject or area of your choosing.

1   Think of a central word, a theme or area of interest that you would like to produce a map on. Write this word in the middle of the page, which you have arranged in a landscape fashion, and draw a boundary around it.

2   Keeping the page horizontal, draw lines or branches out from the centre, and on these lines write single words that you associate with the central image or theme. Remember, write only one word per line. If you think of a word that is more closely associated with the word on the line than with the word in the centre, draw a line off this 'radiating' word and write the new word on this line. Similarly, this word may have associations of its own. If so, draw another line branching off it, and so on. Write down any words that 'spring to mind' – try not to select or 'get it right'. Keep doing this until the central image is surrounded by associations. (Aim for 15 to 20.)

3   If you can, find someone to read and explain your associated words to. Explain why you have made those associations. Move your finger over the paper as you do so. If you are working alone, talk through your associations to yourself. Add any new words you think of.

    This is not, as you now know, a model map. What you have is a series of words that you freely associated with your central idea. You will now start organising your ideas into a map.

4   Look at the words you have written on the page. See if you can find words that go together.

5   Look at your groupings of words. What word would you use to describe each group? In effect you are identifying the organising principle for the group. Put another way, you are looking for the main headings of your map. The 'organising principle' word may or may not already be written down. Try to find enough organising principles to encompass all of the words you have generated.

6   Using a clean sheet of paper, redraw your central idea and add the organising principles that you have established around it.

7   Now add the words that you originally brainstormed to the relevant branches on your model map.

8   Add any other additional words that you think of as they occur to you.

9   Now either go to page 84 (**Developing your maps**), or spend some time practising your new skill. Alternatively, you could read and try out the other two step-by-step guides given below.

Step-by-step guide to mapping, version 2 — the book analogy

In this method we are going to use an analogy: pretend that the topic you have chosen to map is going to be written up as a book. (Alternatively, for practice, you could map a book you know well.)

1   Think of a title for the book and/or a main image to represent the book. This is the centre of your map.

2   Now think what the chapter headings in your book might be. Think carefully before deciding what the chapters are going to be about. Ask yourself questions such as:

    ◆ Would this chapter title be part of a bigger chapter?

    ◆ If so what is this bigger chapter to be called?

    In effect, you are 'revising' ideas about language triangles from earlier in this chapter (page 55).

    Once you have chosen your chapter headings, draw branches out from the centre (remember the advice on page 79 regarding spacing, though with practice you will learn to judge the space you need for each branch). Write the words you have chosen to represent your chapters along these lines.

3   Relate to each of your main branches or 'chapter headings' as if it were a book in itself. What would be the main sub-sections of each? Once you have decided on keywords to represent these sub-sections, draw smaller branches off each of the main ones and add the keywords. Remember an image or diagram can be used at any time instead of a word.

    You now have the title of the book (the centre of the map), the chapter headings (the main branches), and the sections within each of the chapters (the smaller branches off the main ones).

    You may have noticed how each branch exists within, and is enveloped by, the previous one. You may have realised how the work so far in this chapter has been preparing you for this. If you have not read fully the first sections of this chapter, and are finding this difficult to follow, try going back and completing the reading and exercises on pages 51 to 71.

4 Further branches can be added to each of the 'sub-heading' branches, and seen as paragraph headings within the sub-headings, within the chapter headings, within the book.

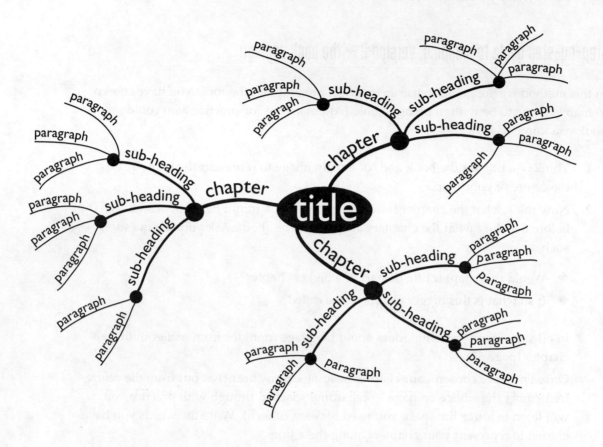

6 Now either go to page 84 (**Developing your maps**), or spend some time practising your new skill. Alternatively, you could read and try out the other two step-by-step guides given above and below.

Step-by-step guide to mapping, version 3 — the literal approach

1 Draw a picture or icon representing the subject of the map. Alternatively, you could use a strong image created with letters, perhaps using drop shadows, unusual typefaces, and so on. Use colour if possible.

2 Decide what are the main categories of information. There will be between 5 and 9 of these main ideas. They are organising principles of your map and may be the most abstract words you use.

3 Use a keyword to 'summarise' each of these main ideas or overarching categories.

4 Take one of these main ideas; estimate how long the keyword will be if written in large letters, and then draw a 'branch' of that length from the central image. Use a chosen colour. Now, write the keyword just above the line, in capital letters in the

same colour as the line. All subsequent and subordinate keywords, lines, illustrations and icons should be in that colour.

5   Concentrating on this one main category, consider what sub-categories you want within it. For each of these, think of a keyword that best and memorably summarises the sub-category. Again, estimate the length of line needed to accommodate the keyword, and draw it in a way that shows it is of less significance than the main idea. You can do this by estimating its length when the keyword is written in a smaller size than the main keyword. You can also emphasise its subordinate value to the main branch by drawing a thinner, less ornate line.

6   Repeat this process for all the first level of sub-categories until all the information you wanted to map has been given a keyword and 'place'.

7   Now, look over this whole branch and see if all the keywords are appropriately categorised. The physical placement is a very visual and spatial way of checking this.

8   See if there are any links you want to emphasise by drawing arrows from keyword(s) to keyword(s). These links may illustrate a relationship not apparent within the hierarchy of categories used.

9   You can now repeat the whole process for each of the other main organising keyword branches.

10 You can deviate from the above sequence, and indeed it's a good idea to do so. These instructions have been written in a linear, sequential way shaping a linear, sequential response from you. This is only needed for your first few maps, as you become familiar with the logic of categories and sub-categories. Once you feel secure in this and the graphic rules used to present them, you are free to deviate – to jump from one spot to any other spot of the map. Simply write down the ideas and keywords as you think of them.

So, if you are struggling or stuck on one branch and an idea pops up about another branch, do not bother to store it for later – use it immediately. This gives you the sense of working 'with the brain', not harnessing it to an unnatural, linear and sequential process. However, you need to master the logic of categories initially. When you do, you will be able to benefit from the power of being both creative and organised.

11 When you have finished, scan your map, looking for sense in the categories and completeness in the details of the outer minor branches. Travel along the branches to test out the logic of the ride.

12 Add to, cross out and redraw your map if needed.

13 Explain your map to someone else, both to check out your understanding and to lock the map into your memory.

Developing your maps

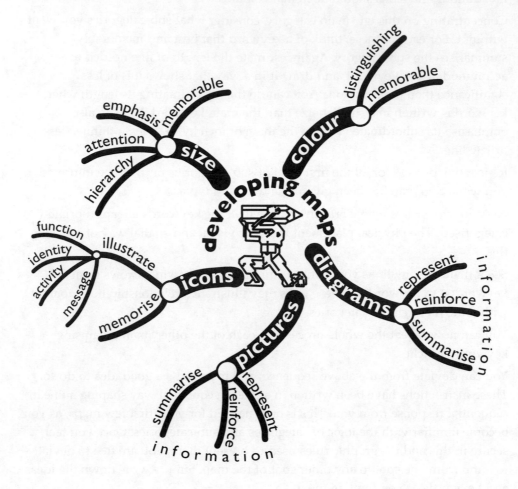

Until now we have concentrated on using words. In fact, we have concentrated on the skill of categorisation and have used words to illustrate the thinking and methodology. You may have already thought about ways in which you can make your maps more unique, memorable and personal. This may aid recall and add interest for yourself as a learner.

Use of colour

Using a different colour for each of the main branches makes them more distinct from one another and aids the recall of information. The use of colour can make images, icons and diagrams stand out from the background.

Use of size

Size can provide emphasis. The most important branches and words at the centre could be larger than those towards the outside. Attention tends to be drawn to the largest words first. These initial branches are the organising principles of a map and encompass the information contained further away.

Use of icons

Icons can be used to summarise a number of words or to indicate a function or activity. They can convey a message and provide something with a unique identity. An icon can convey or carry more information than a single keyword and because of its form can be more readily remembered. You can collect icons, borrow icons, and make up your own.

Use of diagrams

Diagrams are used to provide a visual representation of a significant amount of information. Diagrams can be used to illustrate the workings of something or to summarise the results. Examples of diagrams include bar, flow and pie charts, Venn diagrams and maps!

Use of pictures

Like diagrams and icons, pictures can be used to represent, reinforce and summarise significant amounts of information. You do not need to be good at drawing to include pictures in your model maps. You do need to be clear about what the picture represents to you. The size of the picture should depend on its importance and therefore its location with respect to the centre.

◆ Notes – a model mapper's perspective

For writers, the contrast between linear text and maps is significant. Being based on the organising structure of the topic itself, model maps are created 'out of time'; that is, they are not confined by the sequential and linear nature of time-related delivery of text or aural stimulus.

Taking notes at a lecture highlights this contrast beautifully. However disorganised and confusing the speaker, whatever her manner of jumping around from point to unrelated point, the model mapper proceeds by methodically charting out the major concepts whilst at the same time grouping and organising the details. A discontinuous leap by a speaker is easily assimilated into the growing 'big picture'. Furthermore, subsequent additions can be made to the map that amplify details or themes or links.

Mapping a speaker who is very organised in her delivery – who has organised her talk into sections and her sections into sub-sections – is, however, much easier than mapping someone who jumps about. The point is that a model mapper can cope with the jumping about because he is not restricted to writing in a linear, 'down the page' way. He can jump about with the speaker!

Working in this way is completely different to normal note-taking, which more closely resembles dictation followed by handwriting practice. Model mappers are very active listeners of, and indeed participants in, the lecture. They constantly search to make sense of what they are hearing; turning data into information. By forming hierarchies of categories, they hypothesise whether such conceptual groupings best summarise the topic. And that summary will be shaped by the purpose of the note-taker. A lecture can be interpreted in several ways and so the model mapper will be aware of the need to create a structure that best suits his own 'information need'.

A model mapper may spend some time considering what it is he wants to achieve in order to establish his main organising principles. If his task is to produce an accurate summary of the speech, video or programme, he will try to establish what the main points of the stimulus are. If the model mapper is attending a lecture or course, he may ask the course presenter what the main topics to be covered will be.

Maps, unlike linear text, are easily reformatted or redrawn if new information or a fresh insight opens up the possibility of a new structure. After a lecture, a model map is a very powerful tool to test out your personal grasp of the topic with your fellow learners, or indeed the lecturer. A model map is a perfect basis upon which to ask questions that test both what the mapper thinks he has understood, and what he has not been able to 'place' (i.e. contextualise) onto the map. Model maps are 'public', 'concrete', and 'memorable' in a way that linear notes are not.

Note-making, as opposed to note-taking, is the construction of a plan for writing, public speaking, project creation, or any other pursuit that is your 'invention'. Here, we see a comically similar image of the systematic and vigorous note-taker following the meanderings of an undisciplined lecturer; this time, though, the lecturer is replaced by your own mind.

In traditional note-making, we try to 'discipline' our mind by forcing it to produce thoughts in a sequential fashion, even rejecting good ideas because they haven't appeared in the correct order. The model mapper does no such thing. He accepts all good ideas whenever they appear because they are quickly and efficiently put into convenient and appropriate space on the map. In this way the model mapper works *with* the mind and not *against* it. Whilst being able to deal with spontaneously tempting thoughts, the mapper will find that the visual structure of the model will concentrate his attention on the aspect being examined. It is as if the pattern of the map draws in the attention of the viewer and combines the powers of sight and thought. A real sense of momentum is felt as the categories, links and relationships develop.

In this 'brain-friendly' and productive environment, creativity flourishes. From apparently nowhere, ideas and novel connections appear. It is no wonder that model mappers find both note-taking and note-making engaging, stimulating, interesting and fun. Model mappers, in fact, have an increased capacity for learning.

Review

chapter two

CREDITS

1 What examples of classification can you identify in the area where you are sitting or standing now?

2 What applications of model mapping are immediately apparent to you? In what ways can you see these impacting your classroom practice? Make a note of these now and see if they change after reading each subsequent chapter.

3 What opportunities can you identify where you could practise your mapping skills without it seeming like an additional thing to do?

4 Listen to the news tonight with an A3 sheet of paper and pencil to hand. Map the news.

5 Map your next shopping visit.

Teaching mapping

changing linear learners into holographic thinkers

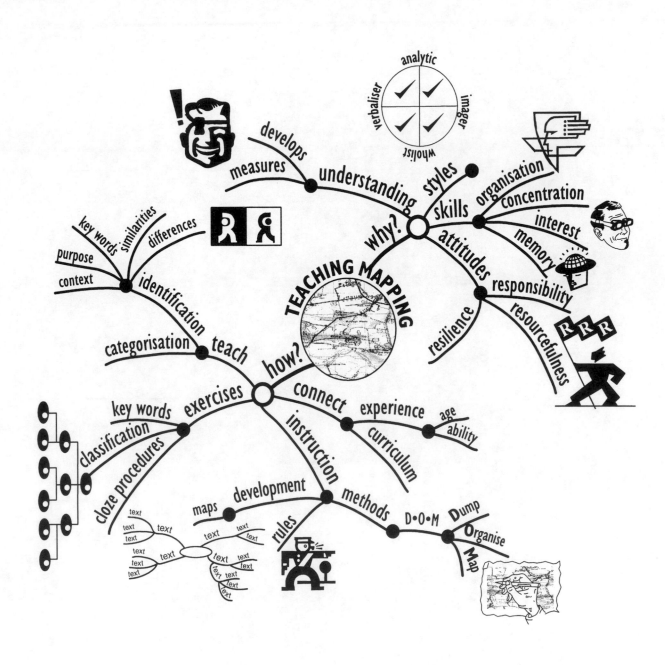

Chapter 3

Teaching mapping

changing linear learners into holographic thinkers

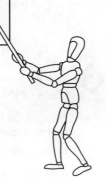

COMING SOON!

1 Why it is important to teach pupils how to produce maps.
2 How mapping has been taught to learners of all abilities,
  in a wide variety of educational and business contexts.
3 More than 20 ways to develop the thinking needed to
  produce maps.

"There is a need to be explicit about what we mean by better forms of thinking and of educating directly for thinking. If students are to become better thinkers – to learn meaningfully, to think flexibly and to make reasoned judgements – then they must be taught explicitly how to do it."

Carol McGuiness (1)

Ian remembers a very early example of someone trying to show him how to read and use a map. This is his story. "I remember, aged 6 or 7, being taken to London to see Buckingham Palace. My Auntie Rhoda tried to teach me how to read the London underground maps. I could understand the ones in the trains above the seats, the ones with only one colour and one line; I enjoyed 'guessing' which station was coming next and grinned when my guess proved correct. But try as I (and she) might, I could not make head nor tail of the multi-coloured, multi-dimensional maps that showed how all the bits went together. It was 15 years before I next went on the underground and I remember two things about this: first, my anxiety about going on the underground

91

without my Auntie Rhoda to show me how to get from London Bridge to Richmond; second, my relief when I realised that I could read and make sense of the big complicated maps by myself – it was easy."

Sometimes realising how easy something is can be really hard and can take a long time.

What follows in this chapter is not, of course, the only way to introduce and teach model mapping to learners. But, having read it, you should certainly be more successful than Ian's Auntie Rhoda at teaching students to think holographically. If this chapter, and indeed the rest of the book, stimulates your own ideas (and perhaps gets more students using public transport!) then it will have fulfilled a wider purpose.

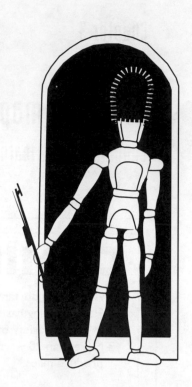

"Tens of thousands of students around the world right now are taking notes. They are writing down words line by line … but the brain does not work that way … It stores information by patterns and associations. So, the more you work in the brain's own memory method, the easier and faster you will learn."

G. Dryden and J. Vos (2)

This chapter is divided into two sections:

◆ Why do it?

◆ How to do it.

◆ Why do it?

It is important to realise, if you have not already done so, that in teaching students to produce model maps you are not merely teaching them another 'study skill' or a 'memory tool' to help them recall information for the next test or examination – although mapping does fulfil these functions. You are making available to them something that will support them in creating meaning and hence understanding for themselves, wherever and whenever they choose to do so, for the rest of their lives.

The learning experience is the responsibility of the learner; it takes place in the learner. By teaching students to map, you are supporting them in taking responsibility for their own learning. You are showing them how they can and do create meaning in the world. It is a gift. It is up to them if they choose to use it. It is up to us as educators to show them what it can make available to them as learners.

In school students are asked to listen to, explore, make sense of and understand the thinking structures and knowledge associated with many different subjects. They are presented with different models of thinking each day. As they move between subjects, they experience the thinking, knowledge and concepts (or at least the teacher's interpretation of the concepts) of each one, which can be very different in nature to the last. In order to understand each subject, students must switch from one way of thinking to another as they move through the school day. Having been exposed to these different stimuli, students are then asked to demonstrate their understanding via essays, notes, comprehension exercises and the like; the standard of work that results can be extremely variable.

> "Children should be at least as self-conscious about their strategies of thought as they are about their attempts to commit to memory. They should be conscious too, of the tools of thought – causal exploration, categorisation and the rest."
>
> *Jerome Bruner (3)*

The essays and answers that the teacher receives are a physical representation of a student's ability to take in, organise, make sense of, and then reorganise into linear fashion, the stimulus that has been provided. Students are not necessarily aware of how they have carried out this process; and this is the point. By teaching students to model map you can show them how they make sense of the world by organising information. Once revealed, this new-found knowledge can be used by your students to organise all future information that comes their way. Unless students know how they make sense of the world – unless this subconscious skill is made evident and available – the standard of work that they produce cannot be regarded in any way as their best.

> "Written or spoken messages are necessarily linear sequences of concepts and propositions. In contrast, knowledge is stored in our minds in a kind of hierarchical or holographic structure. When we generate written or spoken sentences, we must transform information from a hierarchical to a linear structure. Conversely, when we read or hear messages, we must transform linear sequences into a hierarchical structure in order to assimilate them into our minds. Concept mapping can aid this psychological–linguistic transformation."
>
> *J. D. Novak and D. B. Gowin (4)*

93

Model mapping is important because it allows and encourages students to:

◆ analyse and make connections

◆ become better thinkers

◆ learn meaningfully

◆ think flexibly

◆ communicate effectively

◆ become active creators of their own knowledge and frameworks of interpretation

◆ search out meaning and impose structure

◆ go beyond the information given

◆ deal systematically yet flexibly with novel problems and situations

◆ adopt a critical attitude to information and argument

◆ make reasoned judgements

◆ make their own thought processes more explicit.

"Gifted students tend to do this reorganisation on their own, but even they will profit from learning more systematic approaches to organising knowledge, especially ways to see better its hierarchical structure. Less talented students usually resort to rote learning as the only alternative that allows them to maintain their self-esteem in the face of an otherwise almost hopeless learning task. Less motivated students simply give up and become behaviour problems or engage in what Holt (1964) called 'strategies for failure'."

J. D. Novak and D. B. Gowin (4)

The real question, it seems, is not 'Why do it?', but 'What possible reason could anybody have for not teaching children to understand and use model maps in their learning and in life?'

"... [education] needs to emphasise the skills of devising and assessing constructs and techniques, the skills of thinking."

G. A. Woditsch (5)

◆ How to do it

What happened between Ian first going on the underground with his Auntie Rhoda and his return to the tube 15 years later? How did Ian learn how to read and use maps?
This section is divided up under the following headings:

◆ Connecting the learning

◆ Exercises: identifying keywords

◆ Exercises: keywords and language hierarchies

◆ Exercises: organising information

◆ Exercises: from linear to holographic thinking

◆ Drawing their own map

Connecting the learning

In this important first section, students learn that maps are useful, and are introduced to the vocabulary and processes that they will need in developing their mapping skills. The section examines:

◆ Student reactions to mapping

◆ Linking to experience: introducing keywords, selection and organisation

◆ Internalisation of maps.

What follows is intended to inform the way you teach model mapping to your students, though it is not a step-by-step approach that has to be followed in a strict way.

Student reactions to mapping

Unsurprisingly, students react differently to model mapping depending, in part, on their age and experience of schools to date.

The good news is that the authors have yet to work with any students – from year 5 to year 13, and from international MBA students to children with severe, emotional or behavioural learning difficulties – who did not see the value of mapping in the end. Generally speaking, the older the students, the more difficult they can find it to 'give up' established working practices for new methods. An A level student once said he found it hard getting used to the idea that he did not have to write lots of (linear) notes in order to learn. He added that he felt comfortable writing down lots of stuff. When asked if this helped him learn, he said "I don't know, it just feels comforting and I feel as if I have done a lot".

> "… students need explicit guidance in learning about learning and in the tools and strategies to facilitate meaningful learning."
>
> *Joseph Novak (6)*

Other students may find it hard to accept that fewer notes and less writing does not mean 'harder to learn or remember'. There are many variations of this concern, probably associated with students' experience of working in a linear fashion for a significant period of time. Put simply, the older they are the more initial resistance there may be.

PUPIL PAY OFF!

1 less time revising
2 better results
3 homework completed more quickly
4 less time writing
5 more time with friends!

Whatever their age, students will normally be pleased to hear how to spend less time on homework and get better results, so start by focusing on the 'pupil payoff'. Going into the classroom and declaring that 'today we are going to learn a new way of learning called model mapping' and then getting straight down to exercises will be pretty meaningless, and therefore may well meet with a mixed reaction!

95

Linking to experience: introducing keywords, selection and organisation

For all students, try to connect the idea of learning how to map with their own direct experience of maps. With adults and teenage students, look at and discuss maps that are familiar; maps of the locality, road maps or Ordnance Survey maps, for example. With younger children, try studying maps of the school or of adventure theme parks.

Try to draw out specific themes that will be mirrored when you start model mapping. These themes are described below.

◆ **Selection of information**

Information has been selected for the purpose for which the map was designed. Develop the idea of selection by looking at what is not on the map; discuss what things could have been included and possible reasons why they were not.

◆ **Keywords and symbols**

Individual keywords and symbols on the map are used to convey messages, themes and ideas that, once known, carry associations. Explore the use of the information key to develop and illustrate this idea.

◆ **Graphical organisation**

How useful would a map be if it listed the place names but did not show graphically their positions relative to one another? How easy would it be to set out, and to use, the same information in linear form?

Expand on the idea of presentation by looking at the use of font, colour, typesize and spacing, and the effect this has on the reader in terms of providing emphasis and distinction of different areas, functions and purposes.

◆ **Maps are useful**

Discuss the advantages that someone with a map has over someone without one. In general terms, discuss the emphasis that has been given to certain pieces of information on the map, how this emphasis has been given and what the purpose of the map is. Ask why the map has the boundaries it has, and what other maps it might be contained within.

Most importantly, try to develop a sense that maps are useful, and that (assuming we know how to use them) they give us confidence.

When you make a model map - select and organise information

◆ **Make a map**

After spending some time looking at and discussing maps, give students the opportunity to create a map themselves for a specific purpose, to reinforce and demonstrate the learning.

Older students or adults might

create a map giving directions to a party. Younger students could create a map to help a new student find his way around school or the classroom. In each case, the learner is asked to do two things: first, to select the information needed to fulfil the purpose of the map; second, to organise the information so that it is useful. Spend time emphasising these points: that the information chosen is a selection of the total available, and that it only becomes useful once it has been organised.

Internalisation of maps

We all have memorised maps of places that we are familiar with. The students, for example, have all memorised how to find their way around their classrooms, their homes, their school, the locality, and so on. When we go on holiday, we spend the first few hours (or days!) 'getting our bearings' – finding out where things are in relation to everything else.

With older learners, you could talk about how a particular car journey may initially require a physical map. This map gets internalised, eventually, and we soon do the journey automatically (until one day, the road is closed and we have to find an alternative route).

Both a physical map and an internalised one are useful. The ability to read and use them gives us confidence. Ask the learners for examples of other maps that they have internalised. List them on the board, and show that we all use them all of the time. Without them we couldn't find or do very much at all.

Exercises: identifying keywords

We have already introduced the idea that information on maps is selected. Now we want to show how most of the meaning is carried in a very small number of keywords.

The following exercises are intended to give you some ideas and initial ways of demonstrating and teaching this to your students. Some of the exercises themselves will be familiar from chapter 2; here, though, they are set out to show how they may be delivered in a classroom situation.

Exercise 1

Write a sentence up on the board, omitting the nouns, verbs and adjectives. Ask the class to guess what the sentence is about as you write it. Now add the adjectives, and let them guess again. Next, add the verbs, and let them guess. Finally, add the nouns. This is a very easy way to demonstrate that nouns carry most meaning. (The language you use in talking about this exercise will depend on the students' familiarity with the terms 'noun', 'verb' and 'adjective'.)

Ask the students which words they could actually draw. One of the reasons that nouns are easier to recall is because we can 'see' them as well as say them. Adjectives and verbs can only be seen in terms of their relationship to the noun. So, in recalling the noun you are likely to recall the verb and adjective too.

Exercise 2

Students will need paper and pens for this exercise, which can be set up as a paired or group activity. Ask the students to remember a holiday or day trip that they really enjoyed. In each pair or group, they must select one person's trip; set a time limit for choosing it. Then give them some time to write about the day. The idea is for the others in the pair or group to elicit as much information about the trip from the chosen student as they can in the time given. You could make a game out of it, with the winners being the group, pair or individual who has written down the most detail.

To help get the students started, provide sentence stems or writing frames detailing the types of things that they could write about. For example, they could write about the location, weather, people, travel arrangements, feelings, thoughts, funniest/best/worst/scariest moments.

When it is obvious to you that they would be unable to get even a quarter of their information onto a postcard, ask the students to stop writing. Hand out postcard-sized pieces of blank paper, and ask them to write all of their information about the trip on it. When they protest that it is impossible, ask them to put their writing to one side and move on to the next exercise.

Exercise 3

Ask the students to make up their own version of the exercise in chapter 2 (exercise 2 on page 51): ask them to select a passage from a text and identify the nouns, verbs and adjectives within the text. The students could take it in turns to present their chosen passage to the class first without nouns, verbs and adjectives, then without nouns and verbs, and so on. Again, this emphasises that nouns carry most meaning, and also provides practice at identifying the different word types.

Exercise 4 (exercise 2 revisited)

Now go back to exercise 2. Ask the students to highlight all the nouns, verbs and adjectives on their piece of writing about a trip. (As for the previous exercises, if the students are not familiar with these terms, explain and describe the different word types in terms they will understand.) All the highlighted words are potential keywords. Ask the students to consider how much someone receiving a postcard with only these keywords arranged randomly on it would be able to learn about the trip. Ask them what would need to happen to the words for someone to be able to make more sense of them. You are looking for students to realise that, while the postcard would carry a lot of keywords, these keywords have limited meaning until they are organised.

Show an example of a mapped postcard. Depending on your students, you could start working with them immediately to help them organise their keywords into hierarchies and create their own mapped postcards. There is no right or wrong in this. Certainly, you should keep this early work, as it provides a useful resource to return to after students have completed the following exercises on language hierarchies and categorisation.

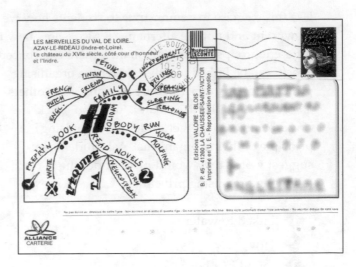

Exercises: keywords and language hierarchies

You may find it useful to revisit the section on language hierarchies in chapter 2 (page 53).

Seeing that words can be placed within language hierarchies will help your students select the words that they need for their maps. The following exercises are designed to help you teach your students that language exists in hierarchies. You will be developing their ability to see higher and lower order relationships between words. In essence, the following exercises contain within them all the skills needed to be a proficient mapper. They are skills we all have to varying degrees. What you will be doing is making them obvious to the students.

"Data are facts; information is the meaning that human beings assign to these facts. Individual elements of data, by themselves, have little meaning; it's only when these facts are in some way put together or processed that the meaning begins to become clear."

William S. Davis and Allison McCormack (7)

It is tempting when you start mapping to think that you need to use lots of keywords in order to record, and therefore remember, information – you don't. The exercises below are designed to help students see how best to select keywords by 'seeing' and using language 'triangles' (see page 55).

Exercise 1

Use Edward De Bono's (8) exercise described in chapter 2 (page 62): ask the students to work out different ways in which these eight different items can be connected by common concepts:

boat	**tree**	**ant**	**duck**
pig	**tap**	**clock**	**cloud**

Use this exercise to demonstrate to students how we can get stuck with an initial viewpoint and not see alternatives. Also, show how the same information can form different groups depending on the organising concept. For example, 'boat', 'tap' and 'clock' can be linked together under the organising principle of 'manufactured by humans' – the others all occur naturally. 'Tree', 'ant', 'pig' and 'duck' could be linked together under the organising principle of 'living organisms'. Ask students to suggest words they would place under the following organising principles:

 linked to water

 large

 found in a house.

>
> "The creative organisation of information creates new information."
>
> *Richard Saul Wurman (9)*

Exercise 2

Ask students what words they would use to describe or group the following collections of words:

 table, chair, bed, sofa

 tennis, badminton, squash

❸ bee, wasp, ant, fly

Use other groups of words to explore categorisation; see if the students can make up some of their own using their favourite topics. For example, ask them to list favourite TV characters, computer games or personalities (TV characters could be a sub-group of favourite personalities). Then ask them to divide the list up into groups or categories. Computer games could be divided up by type, or by manufacturer. TV characters could be grouped into male or female. Ask the students to come up with their own ways of categorising their lists.

When using maps as an active learning tool in the classroom you will see how it is always vital to keep asking 'Is this keyword part of a bigger group?', and 'What words are contained within or under this one?'. Students can start to practise using these questions as they classify and categorise their lists of words.

Exercise 3

Give out sets of cards with the following words on them (or you could use other words or pictures). Split the class into two groups. Tell one group simply to remember the words off by heart. Tell the other group to put the words into groups – to categorise. See which group remembers most.

Apple, Tree, Bicycle, Carpet, House, Stars, Dog, Fish, One, Chicken, Starship, Planets, Pencil, Television, Transport, Banana, Nine, Paper, Tape, Computer, School, Children, Mouse, Car, Pear, Hotel, Seven, Keyboard, Train

Exercise 4

This exercise follows the format of that in chapter 2 (page 59), in which a brainstormed list of words associated with a central them is gradually categorised and placed in language 'triangles' or hierarchies, to form a map. (You may wish students to do this exercise after they have completed the next section on 'organising information'.)
Ask students to think of a central 'theme' word, such as 'exercise' (as used in chapter 2) or 'holiday'. Alternatively, you could suggest a word that will release associations related to a new, current or old scheme of work. Ask them to write this word in the centre of a piece of paper, and draw a circle around it. Then they should draw lines radiating from the circle, far enough apart to allow them to write above each line. Model this for them on the board. Some students will need help drawing the lines.

Now ask the students to brainstorm words associated with the 'theme' word, and write each word on top of one of the radiating lines. (The only reason it is suggested that learners write on top of the lines in this way is that it allows for better use of space; there is no 'brain-based' reason for it.) Alternatively, you could provide your own 'brainstorm' of words.

Take the students through the exercise as described in chapter 2, showing them how to categorise the list of words, and organise them into 'triangles' or hierarchies. Remember to ask them what information they could add at the bottom or top of the triangles. Emphasise that the keywords needed as 'headings' to organise the sub-groups do not have to be contained within the original brainstormed list. For example, the main keywords used to organise the information on 'exercise' on page 59 were not all contained within the original brainstorm. Sometimes we have to go 'higher up' the language hierarchy to find broader, more general words to organise the information most effectively.

Support the students in grouping the words. If they cannot identify a keyword that links or associates a group of words, check to see if the group does in fact go together. Sometimes they will need to move words to another group or start another category altogether.

In the exercises above, students practise the skills associated with identifying keywords, but also begin to classify and categorise information by examining similarities and differences between concepts. Some students find this skill easier than others. The following section will help you to teach the skills of classification and categorisation more fully. These skills are essential if students are to learn meaningfully.

Exercises: organising information

This section is divided up into the following areas:

◆ Organising principles around us

◆ Exercises

Organising principles around us

When working with learners of all ages, spend a little time exploring what it would be like if things were not organised. Discuss and identify examples of organising principles around us. Talk about how the organisation of shops makes our lives easier. Discuss examples of organisation at home; for example, how clothes, food, books and so on are arranged. Schools are very organised places too. For example, most secondary schools have space organised by function and by subject or department. Primary classrooms often have specific areas allocated for specific purposes; these 'zones' are also organised by function. Even teachers' cupboards and students' bedrooms have some degree of organisation!

Exercises

Take your students through the same exercises that you completed in chapter 2 (pages 65–68). (Note that these exercises are available in photocopiable A4 format as a separate workbook – please see page 2 for details. When working with students, it's a good idea to have a set of acetates of the worksheets available.)

"The child recalls a sequence of heaps. She notes likenesses across that sequence. She joins those likenesses in a new representation of experience, a representation more durable and wieldy because it leaves out extraneous sense data. She has formed a complex."

G. A. Woditsch (6)

While these exercises may appear self-explanatory, it is a mistake to assume that everyone will find them easy; even the most able students may find them challenging. Enjoy watching your students learn how they learn.

Organisation of lizards

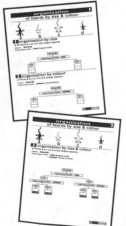

On page 66, on sheets 1 and 2, are four lizards, labelled a, b, c, d. Point out to the students that these represent units of information that need organising. Ask students to do parts 1 and 2 of the exercise to indicate how they could be organised, first according to size and second by colour. Then ask them to complete the third chart to show how they could be organised by size and colour.

With the students, try to think of a real life examples where objects are organised by size, colour or both.

Organisation of monsters

On page 63, on sheets 3 and 4, are four monsters labelled a, b, c, d. Support the students in following the instructions given below the monsters to complete parts 1, 2, 3 and 4.

Organisation of geometric shapes

The series of tasks shown on page 68, sheets 5 and 6, uses geometric shapes as an analogy for information. There are a number of different shapes of different sizes and colours. At present they are not organised or classified in any way.

At this point, emphasise that everything is connected to something else in order for a meaning to be made. Part 1 of this exercise asks students to collect their data. Part 2 asks them to establish the possible principles of classification that they could use to organise the shapes. Part 3 asks them to classify the shapes according to shape, colour and size. Explain the nature of the exercise, and then support the students as they work through each part.

Developing classification skills

The following exercise, which is a variation on those above, is designed to show students that the same information can be classified in different ways depending on the purpose and context.

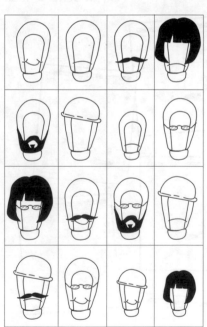

These heads differ in a number of ways – in size, in 'expression', in shape, in the presence or absence of a hat or beard or glasses, and so on. Work with the students as they classify the heads.

Ask students to make up their own selection of different heads or faces, in groups. Then ask them to swap with another group and to classify the selection they are given.

Ask the class to stand together as a group. Ask them how many different ways they can think of to classify themselves: for example, by gender, sport preferences, clothes differences, mode of transport to school, height or physical appearance (eyes, hair, and so on). Ask them to think of reasons why these forms of classification take place. See if they can identify examples of classification in their daily lives at home or at school.

"We have taught classification skills by setting up a role play in which a bouncer on the door at a night-club either refuses or allows entry depending on various criteria, such as style of clothes or shoes. Once in the club, we examined other examples of classification – drinks, music, 'types' of people (age groups, dress codes). A lot of PSHE, Maths and English work came out of this initial fun role play."

Oliver Caviglioli

Exercises: from linear to holographic thinking

By the end of this section, students will have practised using their organisation skills and will have experienced for themselves the fact that a model map is nothing more than a series of key concepts organised hierarchically around a central point. Students will see for themselves that more information can be put down onto paper when organised in this way than through using linear notes. Most importantly, perhaps, by the end of this section students will actually be drawing maps as opposed to writing in linear form.

"The greatest crisis facing modern civilisation is going to be how to transform information into structured knowledge. In order to do that people must overcome their lack of dimension and discover how to make better information connections."

Vartan Gregorian (in 9)

The cloze procedure exercises described below (see pages 69–71) revisit work done to date and give the learner the confidence needed to move forwards.

(Note that these exercises are available in photocopiable A4 format as a separate workbook – please see page 2 for details.)

Taking students through the cloze procedure exercises

Ask students to look at the first mapping classification exercise on page 69, sheet 7.

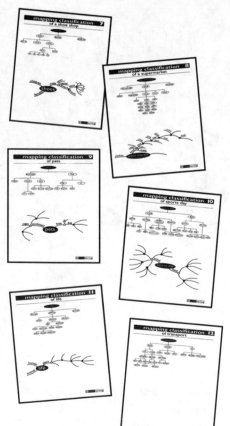

At the top is shown one possible classification tree for a shoe shop. The main classification of the stock is by intended wearer – the shoes are divided up under 'male', 'female' and 'children'. Beneath the classification 'male' the shoes are classified into 'types'; namely 'sports', 'casual', and 'smart'. (The same classification could have been used for 'female' and 'children', but for the purpose of the exercise only the 'male' shoes have been classified.) The classification tree goes on to show the organisation of the shoes according to colour and size.

Below the tree is a model map of the same information. The subject of the classification, 'shoes', is at the centre and the main organising or classification principles – namely 'male', 'female' and 'children' – radiate from the centre. The organising principles of male shoes – 'sports', 'casual' and 'smart' – then branch off from 'male'. Point out to the students that there is room to classify the 'female' and 'children' shoes in the same way here if required, whereas there was little space in the classification tree. Make sure they understand that this is the *same* information represented in a different way.

Ultimately this is what a model map is: a series of key ideas or principles stemming from, and classified around, a central theme or idea. Do not assume that all students will see this automatically; they may not. You are their guide – 'walk and talk' them though the exercises.

Lead the students through the rest of the exercises shown on pages 69 and 70, sheets 8 to 12; they will find other information that has been classified and represented in a model map. Ask them to copy out each map onto a blank sheet of paper. In each subsequent exercise, they will see that more and more information has been omitted from the map. Their job is to fill in the gaps.

"Everyone – teachers, MBA students, 'A' level students, children with moderate learning difficulties, even parents – loves the sense of satisfaction that completing these exercises gives them."

Oliver Caviglioli

As they work through the maps, make sure that they are thinking ahead and check that they are transferring information to the right areas. Ask them how else the information could have been organised.

Drawing their own map

Most students will be ready to start drawing their own model maps after completing the cloze procedure exercises above. Give them the opportunity to produce their own map independently. You could give the whole class the same topic or let them choose.

◆ You may wish to go through the 'rules of mapping' with the students first (page 78). Alternatively you could map these rules onto a board for them to refer to as they draw.

◆ You could let each student draw a map independently, or take them through the process using one of the step-by-step guides on pages 80 to 83.

◆ Model the ways that students can develop their maps using pictures, icons, colour, and so on (page 84).

As they draw their maps, circulate and make a mental note of which students have 'got it' and which students need further support.

Review
chapter three

CREDITS

1 Scan through some of the exercises briefly. Visualise yourself teaching these, or similar exercises, to your students. Make a note of any changes that you would have to make to the exercises or any additional ideas that you have about how to teach the specific skills needed.

2 Picture some of your classes. Visualise ways in which you could use their new skill in
- finding out what they already know
- demonstrating their understanding
- working individually, in pairs, in groups or as a class

Make a note of these now and see if you can add to them as you read the remaining chapters.

3 Think of someone at school who you could team up with to discuss and plan how and when you are going to teach model mapping to your pupils.

Thinking skills

subject to visible thinking

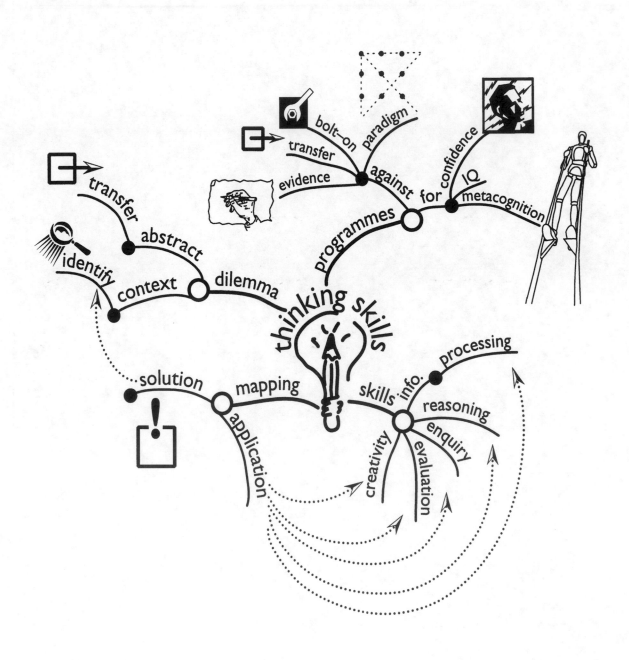

Thinking skills
subject to visible thinking

COMING SOON!

1 How model mapping is one way that all subject teachers can integrate the teaching of National Curriculum Thinking Skills into their subject delivery.
2 How model mapping can be used by teachers to show pupils 'how' they have understood their subject as well as what they have understood by making visible the thinking that is their subject.
3 Why a subject can be viewed as its language and the structure of this language.
4 The advantages and disadvantages of the thinking skills movement to date and how model mapping solves the dilemma about how to teach or integrate thinking skills into subject delivery.
5 How to make thinking visible in your classroom.

"I am very impressed by the growing evidence of the impact on standards of systematic teaching of thinking skills. This is not about some loosely defined or woolly approach to study skills. It is about the ability to analyse and make connections, to use knowledge effectively, to solve problems and to think creatively. It is about developing mental strategies to take on both academic and wider challenges … All the evidence shows that systematic teaching of thinking skills raises standards."

David Blunkett, United Kingdom Minister for Education (1)

This chapter is divided up into the following sections:

◆ Thinking skills in context
◆ Arguments for thinking skills programmes
◆ Arguments against thinking skills programmes

◆ Subject-specific thinking

◆ Resolving the problem

◆ Model mapping as an arena for subject thinking

◆ Maps and the integration of thinking skills into subject delivery

◆ Thinking skills in context

The teaching of thinking is a real problem. We all value the development of this faculty in our students; we are not clear, however, on the best way to go about making sure it develops.

There are various thinking skills programmes on the market. Their authors claim that students completing the courses are then able to use their newly developed skills in any area they choose. In other words, the students are able to apply the *general* thinking skills learned in the course to *specific* subjects. Unfortunately, the evidence does not support such claims – there seems to be a real problem in transferring abstract and generalised thinking skills to be used effectively in specific contexts. Compounding the problem, at school level, is the fact that since the introduction of the National Curriculum in 1988 there has been little focus on thinking skills, and so the search for a solution has been put on the shelf for a decade. With the publishing of the new National Curriculum we are now seeing a return to the issue of developing thinking skills in students – this time with thinking skills firmly embedded within subject teaching and with each teacher having a statutory responsibility to teach thinking skills (2). The aim is to integrate thinking into the curriculum.

"Teaching thinking … is not an alternative to the standards agenda but a way of taking it forward."

Professor Michael Barber, Head of the UK Government Standards and Effectiveness Unit

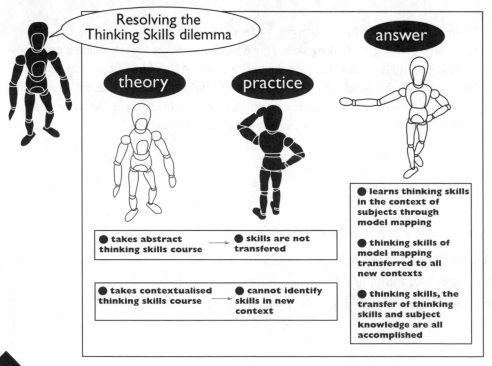

Resolving the Thinking Skills dilemma

theory

practice

answer

● takes abstract thinking skills course → ● skills are not transferred

● takes contextualised thinking skills course → ● cannot identify skills in new context

● learns thinking skills in the context of subjects through model mapping

● thinking skills of model mapping transferred to all new contexts

● thinking skills, the transfer of thinking skills and subject knowledge are all accomplished

Model mapping provides a simple solution to the problem of how you can embed thinking skills into subject knowledge. Since the mid 1970s, the benefits of model mapping have been almost entirely focused on its brain-friendly processes and its capacity for creativity. However, perhaps even greater benefit lies in the way the analytical and organisational skills needed to map in turn lead to the development of thinking skills. To demonstrate the elegance of the model mapping solution, this chapter looks first at the arguments for and against the use of separate thinking skills programmes.

◆ Arguments for thinking skills programmes

The attraction of teaching thinking skills directly has been pursued since the times of Socrates and Plato. If only we could pass on these essential thinking processes to our students, the argument runs, they would be empowered to create a deeper understanding of the information presented to them.

Indeed, the most fervent proponents of what has become known as the 'thinking skills movement' consider that a learner equipped with essential thinking skills will be able to process any kind of information, whatever its content (2). Just as a well trained mechanic equipped with the principles of how engines run is able to work on any make of car, so the student trained in thinking skills will be able to make sense of any subject content.

Continuing the motor metaphor, Edward de Bono, creator of many thinking skills programmes, books and ideas, proposes that thinking can 'boost' intelligence: "Innate intelligence or IQ can be compared to the intrinsic power of the car. The skill with which this power is used is the skill of thinking. Thinking is the operating skill through which innate intelligence is put into action. A high intelligence may be allied to a high degree of thinking skill, but this is not necessarily so. Conversely a more modest intelligence may be accompanied by a high degree of thinking skill" (3).

The strategies used by thinking skills programmes

The potential rewards of thinking skills are only possible if the specific *skills* of thinking can be separated from the *content* of the thinking. By examining what happens underneath the content of subject matter and behind the organisation of subject knowledge, thinking skills can be isolated and analysed.

When this task is completed and the thinking skills are stripped of their context, another background is needed for them. Within a thinking skills course called *Instrumental Enrichment* (4), abstract psychological test materials are used for this purpose on the basis that "… their remoteness from everyday life and other curriculum areas is a strength by enabling the child to become aware of essential process issues without being distracted by subject matter content" (5).

111

By contrast, other thinking skills programmes do not use such neutral content matter. Edward de Bono's CoRT programme (6) uses everyday situations to illustrate aspects of organisation, interaction, creativity and so on. Matthew Lipman's *Philosophy in the Classroom* (7) uses specially written fiction to stimulate discussion that has a distinctly philosophical, rather than psychological, feel to it. In all instances, however, the learner is required to transfer the skills learned across to other subjects.

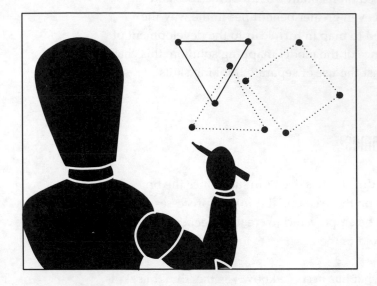

The programmes described above are not British in origin, but British thinking skills programmes have reflected the same range of approaches. The *Somerset Thinking Skills* programme (8) has been influenced by *Instrumental Enrichment* in the way that it focuses on clearly distinguished and psychologically determined thinking processes. Its main difference is that it does not use abstract and neutral content but rather, in the spirit of de Bono, uses everyday situations as the backdrop against which to illustrate successful thinking. Also influenced by *Instrumental Enrichment*, *Top Ten Thinking Tactics* (9) is almost an anglicised and abridged junior version of it.

The telling and subsequent discussion of children's stories has also been used as a stimulus for thinking. Mike Lake's (10, 11) and Robert Fisher's (12, 13) stories are simpler, shorter and more accessible British versions of Matthew Lipman's American philosophical narratives.

The enormously innovative work of Karin Murris (14) took another approach to teaching thinking skills in a philosophical context. More than a decade ago, Murris used 'real' books as the stimulus for philosophical enquiry among very young children. More recently, Robert Fisher has written a series of books using different activities, such as stories (15), poems (16), games (17) and pictures (18), as the impetus for thinking.

Contrasting to the above was *Sharp Eye* (19). This 1988 junior school programme was topic-based and stood out by virtue of its entirely different approach. It embedded thinking skills into the everyday activities of its topics and, as such, was probably not considered to be a thinking skills programme at all by purists. Because of the way it infused thinking skills into the very material it was teaching, it was probably a decade ahead of the game.

◆ Arguments against thinking skills programmes

There is a trend towards using real-life or fictional contexts for illustrating and developing successful thinking. This moves away from the abstract, IQ-type exercises of *Instrumental Enrichment* and represents an attempt to resolve the problem of generalising skills.

If you use abstract contexts in order to focus on essential thinking, you then have to transfer the skills learned to subject contexts. This puts the burden entirely on the teacher of the thinking skills programme to 'bridge' the skills into other contexts. Indeed, this procedure is so central to the success of *Instrumental Enrichment*, that Feuerstein emphasises that his teachers should spend at least half their time doing this. However, this is a very difficult task, and one in which many teachers may feel inadequately supported.

Unfortunately, research confirms that this transfer of thinking skills into other contexts is not happening in the classroom. While thinking skills programmes do have an effect on students' sense of themselves as thinkers and on teachers' sense of themselves as cognitive developers (5), they do not have an effect on raising standards in specific school subjects. The outstanding exceptions to this trend are *Cognitive Acceleration in Science Education (CASE)* (20), and its partner *Cognitive Acceleration in Mathematics Education (CAME)*. Here, students are given a specific thinking skills preparation and then use it as part of the subsequent curriculum.

As a response to the problem of abstracting general thinking skills, other programmes embed their skills in specific contexts. This works well within the confines of that specific context. It makes it harder, however, to identify which aspects of the newly learned thinking skills can be used elsewhere. Perhaps it is not possible. Learning theorist David Ausubel (21) summarises the situation with insight when he writes: "… from a purely theoretical standpoint alone, it hardly seems plausible that a strategy of inquiry that must necessarily be broad enough to be applicable to a wide range of disciplines and problems can ever have, at the same time, sufficient particular relevance to be helpful in the solution of the specific problem at hand." Put simply, for a skill to be general enough for it to be used everywhere it cannot be specific enough to be used anywhere.

So, we are left with what seems an insoluble problem. The more abstract the programme the better able you are to identify general skills but the harder it is to transfer them. The more specific the programme, the less easily identifiable are the general features of the thinking skills. Before we go on to see how model mapping resolves this situation, let us look at the arguments against specific thinking skills because within them lies the basis for a breakthrough in the current approach.

◆ 113

The very term 'thinking skills' is problematic

Let us examine the term 'thinking skills'. It is, claims philosopher John McPeck (22), as vacuous a term as it is attractive. There is as little sense in teaching 'thinking' skills, he claims, as there is in teaching 'winning' skills. Winning cannot be abstracted from its context in any meaningful sense. Can you imagine, after all, taking part in a 'winning skills' programme and hoping successfully to apply your learning to activities as contrasting as chess, marathon running and Sumo wrestling? The activity and the context are inextricably linked.

Similarly, in order to think, you must be thinking of something. 'Think', after all, is a transitive verb, and so it must have an object – you must always be thinking *about* something. When thinking about something, the nature of that subject will govern the nature of the thinking.

Continuing his biting and resonant criticism, McPeck points out that the very premise of the 'thinking skills movement' is based on what he calls a 'trivial pursuit' notion of knowledge. Knowledge is treated as being constant and unproblematic – mere 'stuff'. Only with this simplistic conception can thinking skills take on any plausibility.

Such a mistaken conception of knowledge was made possible by the creation of a false dichotomy, McPeck argues: it is invalid to take knowledge and thinking to be separate entities; they are not separate, but inextricably linked. You cannot think without thinking about something. Equally, you cannot grasp the content of a subject without thinking. It is therefore a literal nonsense to talk of 'knowing how' as opposed to 'knowing that' – you cannot separate the two.

"Learning and reasoning skills develop not as abstract mechanisms of heuristic search and memory processing. Rather, they develop as the content and concepts of a knowledge domain are attained".

R. Sternberg (23)

McPeck traces one possible cause of this misconception to philosopher Gilbert Ryle's (24) distinction "knowing how versus knowing that". If you were unaware of this misconception, it would be valid to think that "… if there were a set of general teachable skills, which we could apply across the board, then we could simply arm students with these skills and turn them loose to face the complicated world" (21).

We all want to believe that thinking skills can be taught directly and no amount of evidence to the contrary will apparently deter us from this view. Indeed, it is interesting to see that some giants in the field of cognitive psychology accept the claims of the thinking skills proponents. Robert Ornstein, for example, who worked with Nobel prize winner Sperry, writes in his book *New World, New Mind* (25) as if it is a fact that *Instrumental Enrichment* (4) raises youngsters' IQ scores. The lure to believe in what can be termed the propaganda of the thinking skills movement is very strong, evidently.

If thinking is content-free, then in what sense is it any different to IQ? And consequently, how can thinking be taught, given the lack of real success in raising IQ scores? Additionally, despite de Bono's assertions (3), we don't find people with high 'thinking scores' and low IQ scores, nor vice versa. Indeed, we find that there is such an overlap in the content of some thinking skills programmes with IQ test materials, that the training becomes, in effect, coaching for the IQ test through content familiarisation. We also find that effective thinkers in some arenas are not usually successful in others – Einstein was not a distinguished poet, for example.

There is an analogous situation in the sporting world. International stars in one sport do not usually excel in others, even if they are physiologically closely-related activities. World-class rowers do not usually become equally accomplished cyclists, for example.

◆ Subject-specific thinking

So, thinking does not take place in a vacuum. You cannot separate the content of your subject from the 'thinking of your subject'. Each particular subject has a way of thinking, and this thinking is shaped by the language of the subject.

The fact that the relationship between subject content and subject thinking has remained unacknowledged has led to what some supporters of the thinking skills movement have called "the miseducation of the last 400 years" (21). It is not that subject-specific thinking is any different in essence from isolated thinking skills, simply that subject-specific thinking is more 'real', as the content shapes a particular type of thinking through its subject language – something that cannot occur in abstract thinking programmes. Below, the thinking behind this position is set out.

One of the premier philosophers of the twentieth century, Ludwig Wittgenstein, proposed that there are 'forms of life' and that these domains of existence have their own particular 'language games'. Furthermore, he asserted, all thought is based in language. These different forms of life, having their own language games, consequently produce different types of thinking. As McPeck (22) concludes "… there are almost as many distinguishable logics, or kinds of reasoning, as there are distinguishable kinds of subjects". In other words, your subject area has its own language and thinking skills. In order to improve the thinking skills of your students, you need to improve their knowledge of and use of the language associated with the discipline.

Another philosopher, Postman (27), makes this remarkably clear when he says: "As one learns the language of a subject, one is also learning what that subject is. It cannot be said often enough that what we call a subject consists mostly, if not entirely, of its language. If you eliminate all the words of a subject, you have eliminated the subject. Biology is not plants and animals. It is language about plants and animals. History is not events. It is language describing and interpreting events. Astronomy is not planets and stars. It is a way of talking about planets and stars."

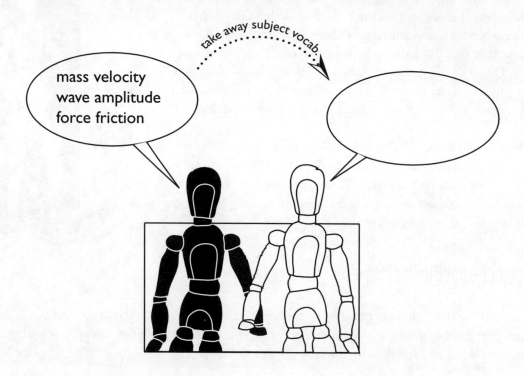

The specialised language of a subject is the key to the development of subject-specific thinking. As leading curriculum designer Jerome Bruner (28) pointed out decades ago, subjects have key concepts, which are the building blocks of our ability to talk about the subject, and to make distinctions and form links and relationships within it.

"Let [a subject] be taught in such a way that the student learns what substantive structures gave rise to the chosen body of knowledge, what the strengths and weaknesses of these structures are and what some of the alternatives are which give rise to alternative bodies of knowledge."

J. J. Schwab (29)

As a teacher, the language and key concepts of your subject are very familiar and comfortable to you. Clearly, however, there has been no opportunity for teachers in general to make these subject-specific thought structures and rules explicit – hence the appearance of thinking skills programmes 'by default'. As the next section explains, mapping can play a key role in making this subject-specific language and thinking available – and, indeed, teachable by all teachers to all students.

◆ Resolving the problem

Since thinking skills are developed within specific subjects, it follows that it is the responsibility of the subject teacher to teach thinking skills. In fact the National Curriculum now *obliges* teachers to teach thinking skills within each subject. The advantage of this approach is that the teaching of thinking skills will not be a 'bolt on' task (5) since each teachers will be 'on their own turf'. Teachers are asked to take on an extra dimension of their chosen discipline, and consequently, it is hoped, subject teaching will improve and standards will be raised.

"We do not think in a linear, sequential way, yet every body of information is given to us in a linear manner. Even language structure is basically linear … we are taught to communicate in a way that is actually restricting our ability to think, because we think in an associative way. When we read a sentence we do not limit our intake of information to what we see in that sentence. We actually make innumerable associations with our own experience. We read in ways we do not write."

Peter Bradford (in 30)

This now begs the question of how exactly teachers are to accomplish this. How can you make explicit, in a variety of modalities, the basic structure from which your descriptions and explanations originate? How can teachers 'give away' their organising principles? How can they communicate their grasp of their subject, which makes their consequent understanding and retention of information so easy and invisible? This is the pedagogical problem that must be addressed if we are to resolve the apparent division between developing thinking skills and subject teaching.

◆ Model mapping as an arena for subject-specific thinking

Before you can produce a model map you need to be able to do two things. First, you need the knowledge and skills of mapping. Second, you need a knowledge and an understanding of the content to be mapped.

key thinking skills
- analyse and make connections
- use knowledge effectively
- solve problems
- be creative

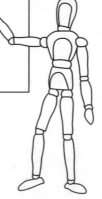

Chapter 2 provides exercises that make the knowledge and skills of mapping explicit. These skills can be summarised as identifying similarities and differences as a prelude to being able to categorise. Thinking skills author Mike Lake (31), clarifies this: "Trying to avoid the pitfalls of over-definition and infinite reduction, I would accept (following both Feuerstein and Lipman) that the essential skills, basic to all subsequent acts of

◆ 117

thinking and learning, are looking for differences and similarities. I use the term 'looking for' rather than 'seeing' to emphasise the essentially active process of successful learning."

These are the skills that underpin the ability to create model maps. Model maps are essentially hierarchies of categories of information, summarised using keywords in language triangles, tessellated and drawn in radiating fashion around a centre and illustrated with images to facilitate memory. Every subject has its own hierarchies of information structured in ways unique to that subject.

> "In the way scientists use language, hierarchies are usually well defined. The fauna and flora of the world … are grouped into sub-species that are grouped into species that are grouped into genera, then into families, into sub-orders, into classes … a vast comprehensive hierarchy."
>
> *James Britton (26)*

The teacher's job is to support students in identifying relationships by comparing new information with what they already know. Three central skills – making comparisons, analytical perception and categorisation – can be successfully taught in isolation and quickly put to use in the formulation of model maps.

Maps themselves cannot be created without content. In addressing the essential nature of the material to be mapped, the skills of making comparisons, analytical perception and categorisation are put to use. And in the process the past knowledge of the student and the characteristics of the language game (rules and distinctions) of the subject meet. It is here, at this juncture, that thinking skills become infused within the separate intellectual culture of the particular subject.

The inherent discipline of creating model maps, along with the visual, concrete and explicit nature of the maps, provides a highly effective vehicle in which subject thinking can occur. Through the process of mapping, students come to understand the content. As the thinking is so visual and easy to communicate, it is open to presentation, interrogation and discourse by both teacher and student. As described in chapter 5, mapping provides a way of creating a new relationship based on partnership between the teacher and the learner.

central skills
"It is only through spontaneously making comparisons that children (or adults) can be modified by the arrival of new stimuli. They have to organise new experiences according to how they can relate to them and compare them with what they already know and think. Relationships are established through comparison." Mike Lake

Chapter 6 shows how creating model maps becomes not only the means to understand the nature of the subject content, it also becomes the means by which the teacher can assess the student's understanding; you cannot successfully map something you don't understand. In addition, the process provides the means to express doubts and clarify distinctions, as well as offering the ultimate memory tool because of the unique visual nature of each map – all within the cultural paradigm of the specific subject being studied.

◆ Maps and the integration of thinking skills into subject delivery

In the United Kingdom, the new National Curriculum sets out what the teaching profession is to understand by the term 'thinking skills', and states that the teaching of thinking skills is now a statutory responsibility of all teachers across all subjects. Despite claims to the contrary, the majority of teachers (particularly in secondary schools), through no fault of their own, do not currently have an awareness or facility to develop thinking skills as part of subject teaching. That is not to say that it does not happen; simply that it is not always explicit, at present. Model mapping can ensure that thinking skills are incorporated into subject teaching.

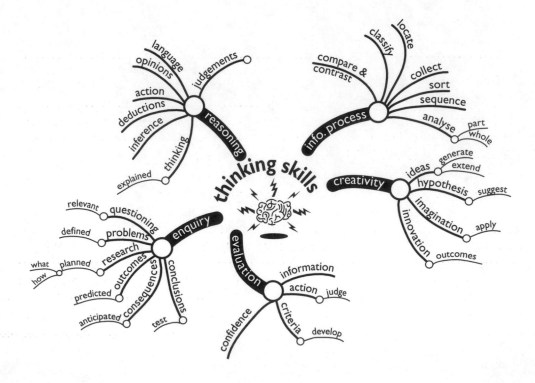

The table opposite which continues overleaf, details how model mapping can be used to support the development of the thinking skills components described in the National Curriculum. Model maps are, in fact, a direct expression of these skills. For example, chapter 5 shows how model maps support students in asking relevant questions, while in chapter 6 we see how they support students in planning what to do ('Enquiry skills'). The components listed in the table under 'Information processing skills' and 'Creative thinking skills' – which are central to mapping – could be seen as the essential thinking skills since without these the other skills are far less likely to take place.

"Focusing on thinking skills in the classroom is important because it supports active cognitive processing which makes for better learning. It equips students to go beyond the information given, to deal systematically yet flexibly with novel problems and situations, to adopt a critical attitude to information and argument as well as to communicate effectively."

Carol McGuiness (32)

Model mapping can no longer be seen simply as an effective means of making and taking notes, or as a technique for students with specific learning difficulties, or indeed as something for the most able. Model mapping is for *all* students: it shows them how they learn and it teaches them how to learn. It does this because it makes evident, supports and develops their thinking skills. It places thinking at the heart of the curriculum because it supports the teachers' explanation and the learners' understanding.

Table of National Curriculum Thinking Skills (continued overleaf)

Thinking skills components	Using model mapping to develop these skills
Information processing skills These enable students to:	
◆ locate and collect relevant information	Model mapping requires the learner to practise and develop these skills.
◆ sort	Information must be sorted in order to place it on the model map.
◆ classify	Model mapping requires the learner to decide on the nature of the classification. This will depend on the purpose and context for which the map is being drawn.
◆ sequence	Once drawn, model maps support sequencing of material since the learner is always able to see the whole and the parts at the same time.
◆ compare and contrast	No longer restricted by linear notes, the learner is supported in comparing and contrasting information as the map is being created. Because all elements of the problem or question can be viewed simultaneously, further comparison is possible once the model map is complete.
◆ analyse part–whole relationships	Model mapping's unique visual and organisational qualities enable the learner literally to see relationships between the parts and the whole simultaneously.
Reasoning skills These enable students to:	
◆ give reasons for opinions and actions	Reasons and opinions may be presented on the map. Equally, evidence to promote or support an opinion or action can be presented.
◆ draw inferences and make deductions	Model mapping supports the learner in making informed inferences and deductions based on the principles underlying the categorisation.
◆ use precise language	Model mapping requires the learner to identify key vocabulary. The vocabulary will range from specific descriptions on the outer branches to more general and abstract terms on the central, organising branches.
◆ explain what they think	Model mapping offers a visual way of showing and explaining what the mapper is thinking.
◆ make judgements and decisions informed by reasons or evidence	The learner can use evidence and reasons made visible by model mapping to make informed judgements and decisions.

Thinking skills components	Using model mapping to develop these skills
Enquiry skills These enable students to:	
◆ ask relevant questions	Model mapping when used by the teacher enables students to focus on relevant detail. When used by the learner, the process of model mapping promotes relevant associations and reveals irrelevancies.
◆ pose and define problems	The process of model mapping will make visible whatever evidence or support material the learner requires to explain her thinking.
◆ plan what to do and how to research	Model mapping promotes thorough planning and research because it supports categorisation and organisational skills. The white space on maps encourages additions and amendments.
◆ predict outcomes and anticipate consequences	Model mapping, by making the 'big picture' available to learners, makes it easier for outcomes and consequences to be considered.
◆ test conclusions and improve ideas	Model mapping provides the learner with a way of judging his thinking against the original 'big picture' and evaluating the 'match'. The format of the map also offers scope for easy alterations and additions.
Creative thinking skills These enable students to:	
◆ generate and extend ideas	Model mapping encourages the generation and extension of ideas because the learner does not have to associate ideas in a linear fashion — it supports holographic thinking.
◆ suggest hypotheses ◆ apply imagination ◆ look for innovative outcomes	Being able to see the whole and the parts simultaneously supports the learner in suggesting hypotheses. A map is itself a hypothesis — an assertion, whose accuracy can be judged against the field of study.
Evaluation skills These enable students to:	
◆ evaluate information	With all aspects of information available and considered, an informed evaluation is possible.
◆ judge the value of what they read, hear and do	Model mapping can help learners to identify criteria for judgement and build an evidence base for informed judgements.
◆ develop criteria for judging the value of their own and others' work or ideas	Criteria can be mapped out and developed through discussion of the model map.
◆ have confidence in their judgements	Judgements can be based on organised and complete models of thought.

Review

chapter four

CREDITS

1 Consider your own subject area. What language is specific to your subject? What would the subject consist of if you did not have this language?

2 Consider how the language of your subject is organised. What hierarchies of language can you identify within your subject area?

3 Think about the level of awareness that your students have about
  ■ the language that is specific to your subject
  ■ the way this language can be organised into hierarchies.

4 Look at the National Curriculum thinking skills as set out earlier. Consider
  ■ where in your subject delivery you would be able to focus and develop these skills
  ■ how using model maps would help your explanations.

◆ Teaching and learning systems

wising up communication between teachers and learners

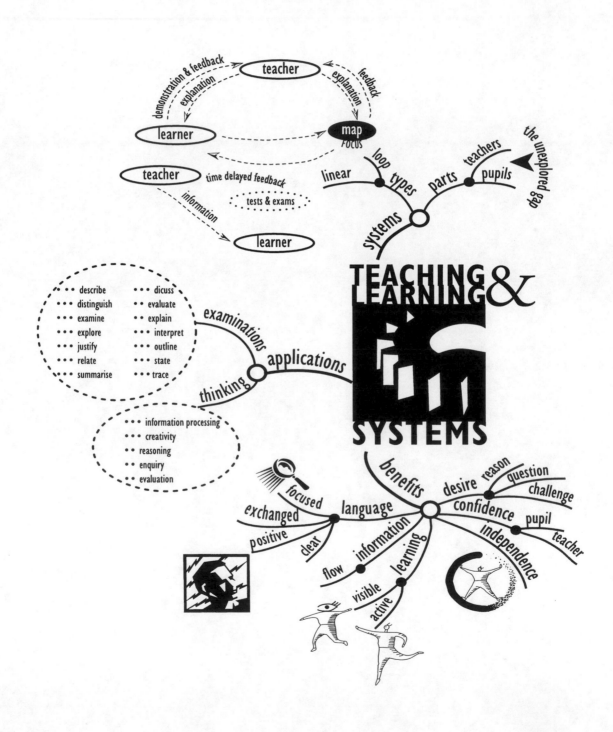

Chapter 5

Teaching and learning systems
wising up communication between teachers and learners

COMING SOON!

1 Two models for examining the effectiveness of communication between teachers and learners in the classroom.

2 What a positive feedback loop is and why it is a good idea to have one in your classroom.

3 How to create a positive feedback loop using model mapping in the classroom.

4 How you can use model mapping to explain and teach key examination vocabulary.

"… we are used to understanding the communication between teacher and learner as the teacher teaching the learner. Seen like this, it looks like a one way, linear relationship, defined by the role. But we could look at it another way. The teacher could not teach without feedback from the learner, as the teacher only knows what to do next by the learner's response. The learner's questions, answers, and expressions, both quizzical and satisfied, let the teacher know how to proceed. So the learner elicits from the teacher exactly what they need to learn. The better the learner does this, the more skilful the teacher appears. In that sense, the learner 'teaches' the teacher how to teach. And the teacher learns how to teach from the interaction. This way of understanding is different from the normal, but just as valid. Here is the origin of the saying 'the best way to learn a subject is to teach it'. Both teacher and learner respond to feedback in the moment and this leads to a virtuous feedback loop."

J. O'Connor and I. McDermott (1)

When someone responds to your outline of an idea or proposal by saying, 'I see what you mean', are they agreeing with your proposal? Not necessarily – it's a neutral statement. Can you assume that they have successfully grasped the essence of what you have said? Not really – you do not know exactly what they have 'seen'.

Nevertheless, people often relate to such feedback as comforting, informative and useful. Spurred on by this apparent agreement you might carry on, embellishing the image on the canvas of the listener's mind. You might imagine that this communication is 'clean' and complete, transferring faithfully the picture in your own mind directly into the imagination of your listener, like a digital transmission. Everything seems fine, until the listener's actions suggest that, despite his assertions, he hasn't actually understood a word. He definitely 'saw' something, but unfortunately it probably wasn't what you were describing.

This chapter examines the nature of the exchange of knowledge in the classroom. To help you find your way around, it is divided up into the following sections:

◆ Identifying the system in place in your classroom
◆ Developing a positive feedback loop using model mapping
◆ Using the loop to develop key thinking skills

◆ Identifying the system in place in your classroom

If we accept Robert Fisher's view that "we live in a mosaic of disconnected bits of experience" (2) what can we do to help students put the mosaic together?

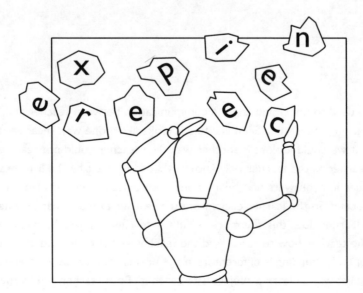

O'Connor and McDermott define a 'system' as "an entity that maintains its existence and functions as a whole through the interaction of its parts" (1). Using systems thinking, we could imagine ourselves helicoptering above a classroom examining the whole, the parts that make up the whole, and the connections between the parts. In order to understand how the parts are connected and work together, we must examine the whole system. The system we are going to examine here is the one in operation in your classroom.

The parts that make up the whole in your classroom are you as the teacher, your students and the environment. In this chapter, we are concerned with the human parts – you and your students. An observer looking in at your class would see you doing and hear you saying certain things. Similarly, she would see and hear your students. But what might she see going on *between* these two parts of the system in your classroom?

"... understanding is a product of doing, yet all too often students sit in the classroom and receive, with little being required of them other than listening, writing notes, and completing low level comprehension exercises. They receive large amounts of information but are not frequently required to do anything with it. Consequently, there is little need to think."

Mike Hughes (3)

The quote at the beginning of the chapter describes two different systems: in the 'linear' system there is a simple one-way relationship, as the teacher teaches the learner; in the other system both teacher and learner constantly respond to one another, setting up a positive feedback loop for learning. In reality, most teachers use both systems, though they may spend more time in one than in the other. However, learning is far more likely to take place in the 'loop system'. It may take place in the 'linear' situation but if it does the teacher probably does not know for sure that it is occurring, or the *extent* to which it is occurring – until the student takes a test to find out. Model mapping can support you in spending more time in the 'loop system' described above.

Let us now consider which system represents a 'best fit' for your current practice. Consider these questions:

1. Do you seek to establish what your students already know about a topic or area of study before teaching it?
2. Do you consider your role as being essentially one that involves delivery of the curriculum?
3. Do your students ask you questions when they do not understand?
4. Do your students get an opportunity to demonstrate what they know?
5. Do you constantly try to establish what they have or have not understood?
6. Do you work out the level at which to pitch language?
7. Do you know which elements of your teaching need explaining to your students?

If you have answered 'no' to any of the questions on the previous page (apart from question 2!), it's likely that our observer would generally perceive a one-way 'linear' relationship occurring in your classroom. This is a very common, and completely understandable, situation to be in. After all, it could be said that you are the teacher so your job is to teach the curriculum. The students' job is to turn up, listen, do as they are told, and go home and try to make sense of it all. As the Head of English at a large comprehensive school put it: "It is almost as if we [teachers] are operating independent of any context. We can become completely divorced from any other information or stimulus. Employed to do our stuff, encouraged by examination syllabuses that are content-driven, we can become divorced from our students and their reality of what is going on."

In this 'linear' system the roles are clear. Our observer can see what you the teacher and your students are doing: mostly – though not all of the time – she sees one-way traffic between you and the students. How can a teacher support a student in creating meaning and understanding if the teacher:

◆ does not know what her students already know about the subject

◆ has students who do not communicate learning needs to their teacher

◆ does not know what content has been understood

◆ does not know what language has been understood

◆ does not know what to explain further, or how to go about it most effectively.

"Teachers have been working very hard to achieve what is both impractical and burdensome … to cause learning in students, when of course learning must be caused by the learner … When the goal of teaching becomes the achievement of shared meaning, a great deal of both teachers' and students' energy is released."

J. D. Novak and D. B. Gowin (4)

The teacher cannot teach effectively without feedback from the learner. You cannot know that your explanations are working and that you are extending your student's levels of understanding and skill unless you are sure about what is going on where the learning really takes place – in the learner. Without feedback, teaching is reduced to the dissemination of information (and the management of behaviours that become part of this system) and learning is left to chance.

"If you believe it is your responsibility to get through to students in whatever way you have to, you will become a better teacher. However, if you claim that your responsibility is only to present information and then it's the student's responsibility to understand it, you might as well just mail them a book."

E. Jensen (5)

◆ Developing a positive feedback loop using model mapping

Model mapping has enormous potential in supporting the transformation of the relationships between the learner and his own learning, and between the learner and teacher. In the past, the perceived benefits of mapping have focused on study skills, creativity and memory applications. As important and useful as these benefits are, the opportunities that model mapping can create for the learning process are even greater.

"A map provides people with the means to share the perceptions of others. It is a pattern made understandable."

Richard Saul Wurman (6)

By placing and using model maps at the front of the class as part of your classroom delivery, you can make your thinking (and/or the thinking of the class) visible, and therefore available, both to yourself and to the students. It is as if there is a third party in the room upon whom you and your students can focus your attention, rather than focusing on each other. From your own perspective, you are supported in modelling your thinking for your students.

If you are willing to show students how you have made sense of a problem, or how you have organised some information, so they will be more disposed to imitate you. You are, after all, a role model! When the thinking of the teacher or class is made 'public' in this way, students who might usually find it difficult to participate in class discussions are far more likely to do so. This probably happens for several reasons. First, the map gives these students an external focus for their thoughts, which brings their attention away from any negative internal thought processes ('I

"... maintain an open window on your own thinking processes. Reveal – vocalise – your own thinking ... what you model in the classroom will have the dominant impact on students."

G. A. Woditsch (7)

can't do it'). Second, the map gives students something to say; that is, the map provides key vocabulary and ideas that they can either comment on directly or use as a base for their own ideas. Third, there is already agreement in the room that what is on the board

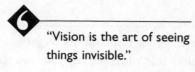

"Vision is the art of seeing things invisible."

Jonathan Swift

is valid or at least valued. Fourth, and most important perhaps, is the fact that your thinking has been captured, frozen, freeze-framed – unlike oral articulation. It is therefore static, 'graspable' and available to your students. For many students, the use of a map will reduce their fear of failure.

Carol Hariram teaches students who have severe learning difficulties, at Woodlands School in Chelmsford. She tells of the difference model maps make to her story telling: "I had two groups on the same day. With the first group I did not have the story mapped in the background. I used props and gave a 'lively' presentation of the story but at the end of the story when I asked questions none of the children could link events or any of the characters together. With the second group we mapped the story as we went along. The difference in terms of their willingness and ability to participate in discussion afterwards was amazing."

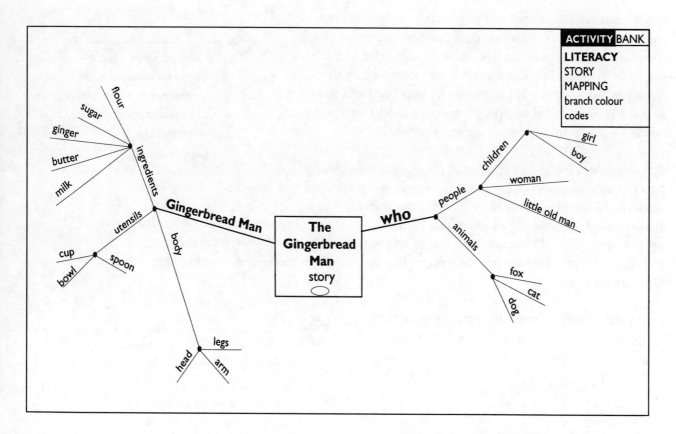

(Note that the above is a summary map for teachers. It represents the much larger, coloured and 'velcroed' map that was used with the students.)

With the first group there was a linear system in operation – the teacher was telling the story and the students listened. With the second group, a positive feedback cycle – a 'loop system' – was in operation. The teacher had developed the children's ability to respond by creating a visual response to the story. How well does this teacher's experience mirror your own?

132

"They [mind maps] automatically inspire interest in the students, thus making them more receptive and co-operative in the classroom."

Tony Buzan (8)

"... as a rule, students do not ask questions in normal practice ... They are busied with other things, notably giving answers to teachers' questions. Classroom discourse normally proceeds in ways that rule out student questions."

T. Kerry (9)

When students have a map upon which to focus, they find it much easier to articulate their efforts to create meaning, and to ask questions. By asking questions the students tell you what they do not know and therefore what you need to teach (explain) next. The map supports the students in examining the learning experience being offered: they have ready access to the knowledge and ideas being presented and built upon, and they have all the information they need to weigh up arguments before coming to balanced judgements. The use of maps makes all of this easier to do and more likely to happen. Together, you and your students can examine the map, change it, add to it and weigh arguments.

"They [maps] stimulate active thinking, develop cognitive skills of analysis, categorisation and synthesis, and provide a visual means of communication and evaluation."

Robert Fisher (2) (reproduced with the permission of Stanley Thornes Publishers Ltd, from Teaching Children to Learn *by Robert Fisher, first published in 1995)*

Model mapping promotes particular attitudes in students. By using maps students develop a desire to reason, they are more willing to challenge and they rediscover a passion to see things through to the end. As these characteristics develop, your students become more self-confident, and what Fisher terms 'critical' thinkers (2). Such students are far more likely to participate with you in the learning process. What may once have been a linear learning relationship develops into a cyclical one; a 'loop system' has been created.

133

"When learner and teacher are successful in negotiating and sharing the meaning of a unit of knowledge, meaningful learning occurs."

Joseph Novak (10)

In case you are not already convinced about the merits of model mapping in promoting a positive feedback system, let us look closer still and consider what such a system in your classroom would 'look like' to an observer. The elements described below do not exist separately from one another within the system, but it is useful to look at them separately to highlight the impact that model mapping can have on the relationship between you and your students.

Conversation

Perhaps the most obvious difference our observer might notice is that a positive exchange of language is occurring in the classroom between you and your students – a conversation.

"Mapping provides a whole language framework in all the areas of language skill – speaking, listening, reading and writing, can be used in useful ways."

Robert Fisher (2) (reproduced with the permission of Stanley Thornes Publishers Ltd, from Teaching Children to Learn *by Robert Fisher, first published in 1995)*

In a linear relationship the teacher does most of the talking and the student is a passive recipient of this language. You may well be very good at explaining what you are teaching, but how do you know that your students are understanding what you say? With a map present, the students can see the structure within which your words should make sense. They also have a structure to help them question what you are saying. They can be specific about what they have or have not understood. They can teach you how to teach them.

"As any photographer knows, the frame of the viewfinder 'organises' the image within it, creating a visual statement where, without the frame, one might get only clutter."

D. N. Perkins (11)

Because they no longer have to interpret what you are saying, your students are freed up to listen to what you are saying. In addition, they are able to use the model that they have examined, questioned and developed with their own ideas as a structure to support their writing.

Flow of information

The second thing that our observer might see is a flow of information between yourself and the students – not a one-day 'dissemination' followed by a delay as they write an essay, complete an exercise or do a test, but an ongoing collaboration of teacher and students.

"Mapping can help information flow to, from and among students and teachers ... Most importantly children learn a procedure for investigating, visualising and organising information."

Robert Fisher (2) (reproduced with the permission of Stanley Thornes Publishers Ltd, from Teaching Children to Learn by Robert Fisher, first published in 1995)

Active learning

Most importantly, perhaps, mapping provides you with another means of ensuring that active learning takes place in your classroom – not formal, direct instruction and not undirected meaningless 'copy-and-colour' activity, but active learning. When active learning takes place, students engage their natural capacities to be interested, curious and co-operative, to enquire and to analyse. We cannot force students to engage in learning, nor should we try to. We can, however provide a system in which they can usefully engage.

"Rather than supporting a passive teaching/learning environment, mapping encourages children to be actively engaged in thinking, to elaborate and build on ideas."

Robert Fisher (2) (reproduced with the permission of Stanley Thornes Publishers Ltd, from Teaching Children to Learn by Robert Fisher, first published in 1995)

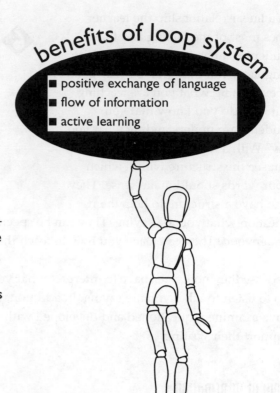

benefits of loop system

- positive exchange of language
- flow of information
- active learning

"If teachers want their young students to have robust dispositions to investigate, hypothesise, experiment, and so forth, they might consider making their own such intellectual dispositions more visible to their children."

L. G. Katz (12)

◆ Using the loop to develop key thinking skills

Model mapping can be used to help students develop some of the key skills they will need as they study in school and tackle examinations.

The table below lists some reasoning skills using terms that are commonly found in examination papers and that are used by teachers. Model mapping can be used by the teacher to illustrate and explain what is meant by this 'examination vocabulary' (13) as it is a visible expression of the skill being developed. It supports the student in carrying out the skill described (see table).

"The sole task of an education system should be to give you the tools and provide you with a critical mind, so that you can ask the right questions, make the right connections."

Richard Saul Wurman (6)

'Examination skill'	How model mapping supports the student in carrying out each skill
◆ **Describe** … give a detailed account	The learner has access to detail and structures underlying the detail on a model map.
◆ **Discuss** … investigate or examine by argument	The learner has a clear structure to support discussion and the map supports the addition or inclusion of new arguments and ideas.
◆ **Distinguish between** … indicate the differences between	The learner can see and therefore point to the differences.
◆ **Evaluate** … give your judgements about the merits of theories or opinions	With all features present the learner can make supported judgements.
◆ **Examine** … look closely into	The learner can analyse all the details.
◆ **Explain** … make plain, interpret and account for; give reasons for	The learner can illustrate her thinking.
◆ **Explore** … examine thoroughly, consider from a variety of viewpoints	The learner can examine thoroughly and can add ideas at will.
◆ **Interpret** … make clear and explicit; show the meaning of	The very structure of the map demonstrates the interpretation. The structure reminds the learner of her thinking.
◆ **Justify** … show adequate grounds for decisions and conclusions	The learner has all the supporting information readily available at the same time.
◆ **Outline** … give the main features or general principles of a subject omitting minor details and emphasising structure and interactions	The learner can see the essential elements and mapping provides the structure.
◆ **Relate** … show how things are connected to each other, and to what extent they are alike or affect each other	The learner can see existing relationships between concepts and can create new ones.
◆ **State** … present in a brief, clear form	Essential language and concepts are evident.
◆ **Summarise** … give a concise account of the chief points of a matter, omitting details and examples	Central branches hold the main ideas.
◆ **Trace** … follow the development or history of a topic from some point of origin	The learner can 'polebridge' her understanding.

So, model mapping can support your students in developing their reasoning skills. This is important for learning, because they reason (or work things out) in order to create personal meaning or understanding for themselves.

"In addition to an increase in production, I have found that mapping encourages students to think in more concrete terms about the concepts behind what they are learning. Model mapping encourages clearer thinking and I have seen a commensurate growth in student confidence because they are more sure of their reasoning. Mapping takes students through each stage of the thinking process and puts an order to it. Instead of following 'will-o-the-wisp' trains of thought and arriving at a conclusion, students can now identify the steps which will lead them there, and most importantly can replicate the process."

Val Hill, Head of English, and Teaching and Learning, Stewards School, Harlow

Review
chapter five

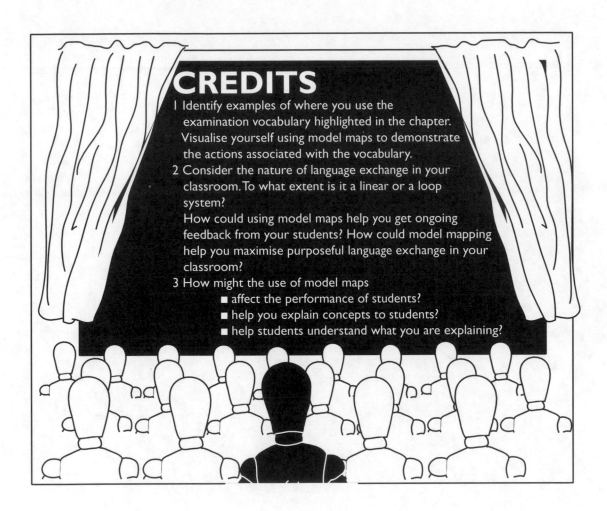

CREDITS

1 Identify examples of where you use the examination vocabulary highlighted in the chapter. Visualise yourself using model maps to demonstrate the actions associated with the vocabulary.

2 Consider the nature of language exchange in your classroom. To what extent is it a linear or a loop system?

How could using model maps help you get ongoing feedback from your students? How could model mapping help you maximise purposeful language exchange in your classroom?

3 How might the use of model maps
- affect the performance of students?
- help you explain concepts to students?
- help students understand what you are explaining?

MAPWISE — accelerated learning through visible thinking

Chapter 6

Maps in the classroom

mapwise classrooms in action

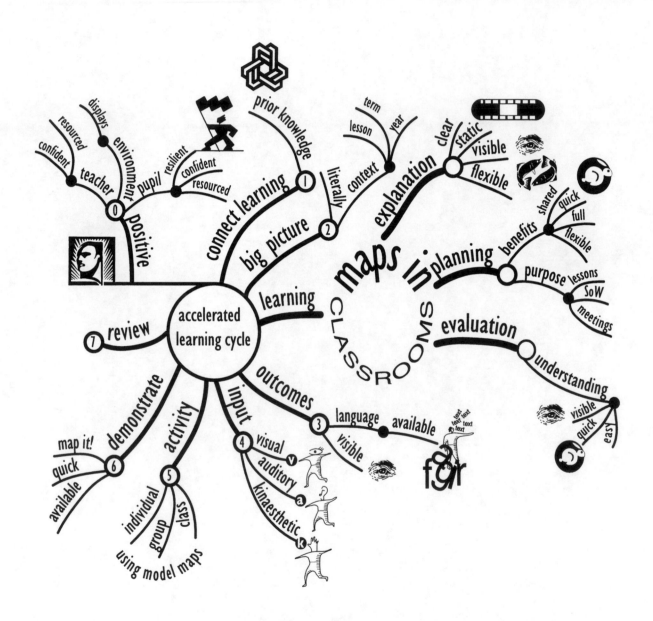

MAPWISE — accelerated learning through visible thinking

142

Maps in the classroom

mapwise classrooms in action

COMING SOON!

1 How to plan schemes of work more effectively.
2 The fundamentals of explanation.
3 Another facet of pupil self esteem.
4 The relationship between teacher confidence and the learning process.
5 How to check pupil understanding.
6 Study skills are boosted by model mapping.
7 How model mapping supports each stage of Alistair Smith's accelerated learning cycle.

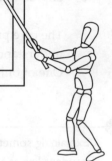

 "How do I get to the Old Kent Road from here?" asked the lost pedestrian. "Well if I were you," came the considered reply from the local, "I wouldn't start from here."

An old joke, no doubt, but how many times have you felt it would be better to start from a different place when you were lost in a sea of information? It is easy to feel overwhelmed and anxious if you cannot establish reference points when working through new material. You need a perspective that will show you the 'big picture'.

When you can see a big picture, reference points are secured and you can make out options for traversing the terrain. A previously confusing mass of information becomes conquerable as its parts are integrated into the big picture through connections to other locations on the map. You begin to make meaning out of previously disconnected perspectives. Understanding emerges.

"Cognitive maps can provide children with a means to articulate their ideas. They provide a tool for planning and assessing or evaluating what they know."

Robert Fisher (1) (reproduced with the permission of Stanley Thornes Publishers Ltd, from Teaching Children to Learn by Robert Fisher, first published in 1995)

"Mapping has been a liberating tool for me personally and for my teaching. It has freed me from a belief that I needed detailed notes on everything in order to remember and understand anything. I am now able to pass on that freedom to my students."

Val Hill, Head of English, and Teaching and Learning, Stewards School, Harlow

This chapter is divided up into the following sections:

◆ Explanation

◆ Planning

◆ Applying maps to the accelerated learning cycle

◆ Explanation

The core purpose of education is to support learners in creating meaning and understanding for themselves. Everything we do as educators should forward this aim. One of our primary tools for this is explanation.

"Explaining something clearly to a student lies at the very centre of a good teacher's professional repertoire."

E. C. Wragg and G. Brown (2)

A dictionary might define the term 'explain' as 'to make plain or clear, to show the meaning of'; this is exactly what a map does.

Effective explanation in the classroom is actually a two-way process. By using model maps you can reveal to your students your understanding about the topic or concepts of the lesson. They can literally *see* what you are saying. By the same token, you can see what they have understood from their own maps.

Robert Fisher (1), identifies some key aspects of what teachers do when they explain a concept or idea to their students (see following table reproduced with the permission of Stanley Thornes Publishers Ltd, from *Teaching Children to Learn* by Robert Fisher, first published in 1995).

Aspect of 'explaining' (from Robert Fisher's list (1))		
◆ Labelling	giving no explanation	things just are – e.g. "this is an orange"
◆ Enumerating	giving odd facts	this is what they are – e.g. "there are oranges in shops"
◆ Making a link	pairing contiguous ideas	e.g. "oranges grow on trees"
◆ Identifying common characteristics	similarities	e.g. "oranges are round" and "oranges have pips"
◆ Identifying concepts as belonging to a class	knowing class name	e.g. "oranges are fruit/food"
◆ Identifying concepts as belonging to a pattern or hierarchy of concepts relating to other classes		e.g. orange as fruit/food/plant/living thing
◆ Identifying concepts as relating to other patterns of concepts	identifying similarities/ differences with other classes	e.g. orange related to linguistic, mathematical, scientific, historical, geographical, economic and other conceptual patterns

Maps can give a massive boost to teacher confidence. By drawing a map you are forced to examine your own understanding and to clarify your explanation. Once the map is done, you need never be unsure about how the content fits together nor need you have any concerns about the students being able to 'see' what you mean.

The message is simple: using maps is an effective way of supporting clear teacher explanation and student understanding.

You cannot start to explain anything to students until you know what they already know. Explanation can only take place when new information is based on and linked to the learner's existing knowledge. If you do not know what they know, you are left making a lot of assumptions about your teaching and their learning.

> "Even very experienced teachers are very often surprised at the fuzziness of their own ideas about a topic they may have taught for years when they take the time to concept map the topic."
>
> *Joseph Novak (3)*

The importance of finding out what students know is illustrated by the work of Wragg and Brown (2). They describe how a student teacher introduced volcanoes to two different groups. With the first group she did not spend any time finding out what they already knew. She introduced the topic by saying, "Today I want to tell you a little bit about volcanoes. Here is a model of one and you can see that this is the crater and, as you probably know, this is the lava, and this part here is called the magma chamber. Perhaps you have heard of volcanoes before. There is one in Italy called Vesuvius …"

With the second group the teacher showed the children the model and asked if anyone knew anything about volcanoes. You will not be surprised to hear that a mass of information came from the group that surpassed what she herself had told the first group. The second group, for example, knew the names of several volcanoes and their locations; they knew that volcanic dust could travel thousands of miles in air streams; they knew about Icelandic geysers and terms like 'lava' and 'eruption'.

With the second group, the teacher was able to establish what they knew and identify the level of language that the group were happy with. She was also able to identify any misconceptions that the students had about volcanoes.

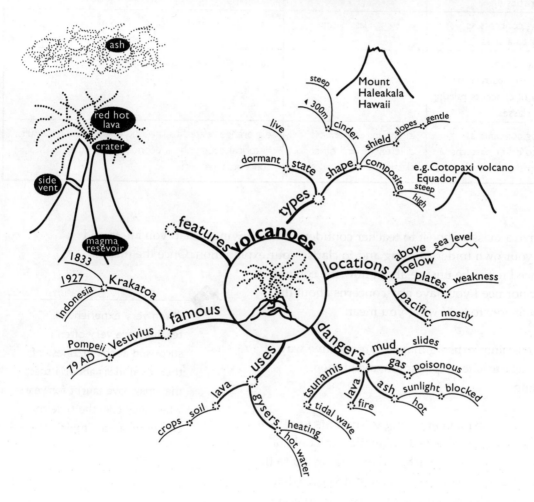

A map can be used to capture the current mental model held by an individual or a group about a particular topic. The work of the teacher above with the second group of students was obviously useful. If she had drawn a model map of their understanding, not only would she and the students have been able to see clearly what they collectively knew, they would also have been able to see exactly how the students' understanding was developing as the topic progressed.

Using model maps produced by a whole class or group is a very powerful teaching and learning tool. You could use the DDOM or the IPSDOM method for doing this. DDOM stands for 'Discuss, Dump, Organise and Map', and involves a class discussion about

146

the topic followed by a random 'dumping' of the information generated on one section of the board. This information is then organised (grouped) before being mapped.

IPSDOM stands for 'Individual, Pair, Share, Dump, Organise and Map', and is carried out in exactly the same way as DDOM, except that the information to be mapped is generated by the students in a slightly different way. First ask the students to think of one, three or five words to do with the topic, before asking them to pair up and compare. Each pair then shares their information with another pair, and then the group of four teams up with another group before the students feedback to you. You then 'dump' the class' information on the board, organise it and map it – all the time discussing with the students how to go about this. In this way, you and the students make sense of the information together, as you create meaning and therefore understanding.

Now that you know what your students know, you can build on this. Explanation is supported because you are providing students with a picture of their growing understanding. If a point is reached where the students do not understand, they are able to use the map to help them explain to you exactly what they do not understand. Because she can see the whole picture and the individual components of the whole at the same time, the learner is better aware of the significance of what she has not understood. The teacher and learner can see this simultaneously.

> "The children do their concept map at the beginning of a unit of work or topic; for example, year 4 did a concept map at the beginning of a science topic on solids and liquids. The children did this as a whole class map initially, and then, once modelled, attempted to do individual maps."
>
> *Mrs. Chowdhury, Year 4 Teacher, St. Clements Church of England Primary School, Nechells, Birmingham*

As you read through the rest of this chapter, keep this key theme of 'explanation' at the forefront of your thinking. In particular, look at how this notion of understanding is cemented in the sub-sections on 'connecting the learning' and 'demonstrating understanding' (see pages 154 and 161).

◆ Planning

This section is divided up under the following headings:

- ◆ Making your thinking public
- ◆ Planning for teachers
- ◆ Planning for students

Making your thinking public

Consider this – as a teacher you aim to give students the product or outcome of your thinking, but do you give away the thinking itself? You have undoubtedly, over the years, got better at selecting and organising the information and strategies needed for your lessons. You also have a strong grip on your subject area generally, its language, structure and the thinking required to create meaning and understanding. You could say that you have become confident and knowledgeable in the 'philosophy' of your subject. How can you communicate this confidence and knowledge to your students?

Teachers successfully give students the benefit or product of their thinking and understanding, but rarely share with the students how they themselves have understood the topic; they often expect students to understand without explaining how they made sense of the content in the first place. This, in effect, is asking the students to

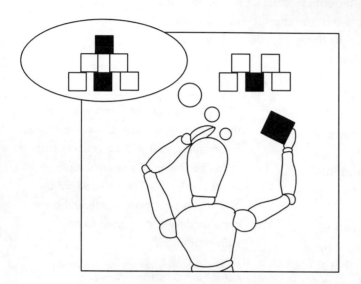

work it out for themselves, from scratch – to do a jigsaw puzzle without the box lid. When you use mapping to set out a scheme of work, a topic overview or a lesson plan, you create a model of your thinking, which is then public and open to examination.

There are, however, two pitfalls in physically demonstrating to your students how you have understood and organised the subject information. First, you must stress that this is only your interpretation of how the information goes together. The usefulness of the model mapping technique lies in the process and not necessarily in the result. Model maps are only models of reality and are therefore only interpretations. This will become obvious when you see the range of different models, or interpretations, of a topic that students produce when they plan projects, essays or presentations using model maps.

Second, your model map may well not make total sense to your students (or to anyone else for that matter) until you 'walk and talk' it through (polebridging). In order for students to understand your thinking you need to take them through it – 'walk' them through it – explaining your understanding of it as you go.

Planning for teachers

The upper map on the next page shows a history teacher's overview of a scheme of work covering the origins of World War II. Notice that the Italian invasion of Ethiopia takes up only a few centimetres of space. The lower map shows how the teacher then expanded on the Ethiopian Crisis by drawing a whole map on it as a single lesson plan.

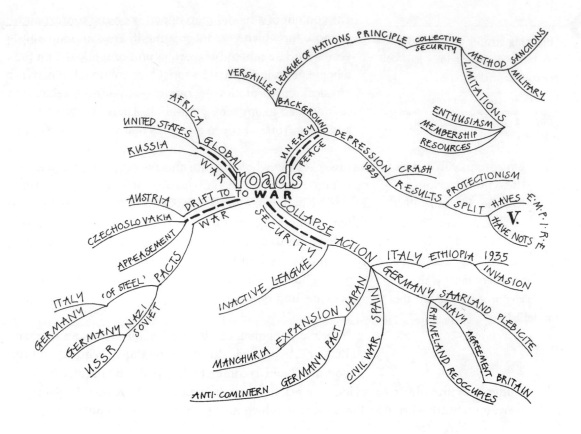

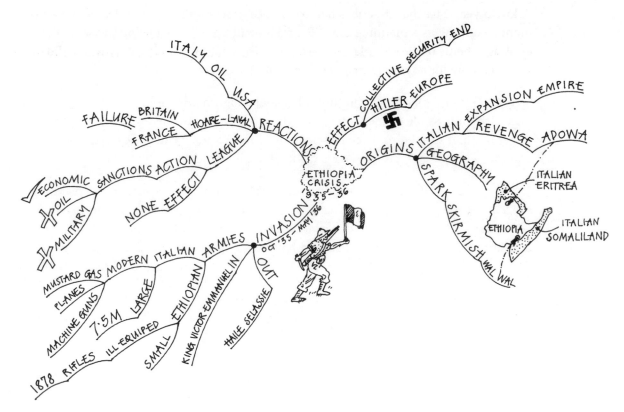

"Mapping strategies can allow teachers to cover topics in greater depth."

Robert Fisher (1) (reproduced with the permission of Stanley Thornes Publishers Ltd, from Teaching Children to Learn *by Robert Fisher, first published in 1995)*

The content of a model map depends on the context and purpose for which you are creating it. You can map a year's work, a scheme of work, a unit of work within the scheme or an individual lesson. Once created, the map is a physical representation – a model – of your thoughts. It can be amended in any way you see fit. There is room for additions. You may even see areas that you want to omit.

On a map, you can simultaneously see the whole picture and the pieces that make up the whole. No longer dependent on memory to keep disparate parts of the topic together in your mind's eye, you are better able to see relationships between the pieces and the whole. You can highlight relationships on the map by using keys, arrows, and colour. Similarly, because you don't need to turn pages to remind yourself of the full story, you are supported in seeing how best to sequence, resource and deliver each scheme, unit or lesson.

"What matters most is the modelling process and not the model."

Ian Harris

Your planning map can be used to fill in any government, LEA or school curriculum administrative requirement that you may have to complete. It can also be used with students to provide an overview of work to be covered and to help reveal the prior learning that they bring to the subject, to which new learning can be connected.

Below, a year 2 teacher describes her experience of working with a colleague who used model mapping as a planning tool. "Before, I would plod along using the school's existing scheme of 'boxed' planning – a non-creative form which, to my mind, didn't seem to allow for any imagination or free thinking.

"At first, I found planning with [my colleague] a nightmare. I found pinning her down was fairly impossible as mentioning the "P" word would throw up a 'rigid system' wall in her brain; it seemed to block her creativity. I used to read categories from the planning sheet to her, but she seemed stifled by the structure.

"After a while, she would wander around the classroom, not looking at the planning sheet, but simply talking about one idea, then another. I'd be sitting, trying to fit her ideas into the boxes, until she'd start to write keywords on the whiteboard, hitting on one amazing idea after another, and I'd have to screw up the paper and start again. Then I realised that if I went along with her and memory mapped the ideas, later I could fit them into the boxes" (4).

Planning for students

When told that 20% of the marks for Business Studies went on planning, a student at Chigwell High School in Essex pointed out politely to the teacher that "nobody has ever taught us how to plan!"

The authors spent three hours with the group, and taught them how to model map. For homework, their teacher asked the students to plan a presentation for the following week based on units of work that they had covered during the year so far. A week later, their A3 maps had been reduced onto overhead acetates and the students 'walked and talked' their maps to their peers. One of their maps is shown here.

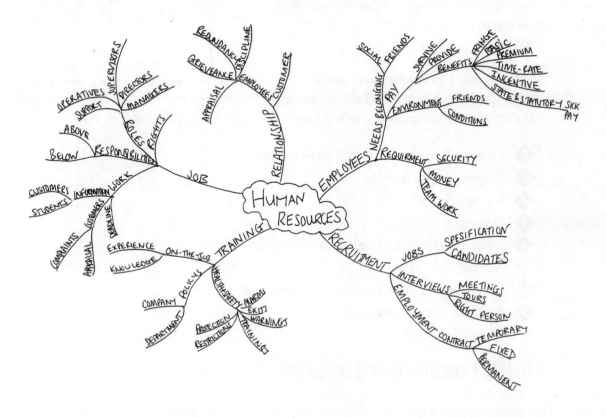

Students can use model mapping to plan any aspect of their work at school and at home. Students who use mapping as a planning tool can expect to find their planning easier and more effective; they can expect to be better able to manage their homework and revision; they can expect to be able to demonstrate and communicate their understanding more readily. At the end of the day, they can expect better examination results.

◆ Applying maps to the accelerated learning cycle

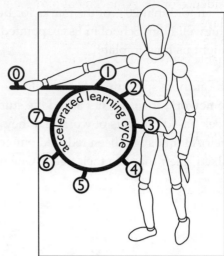

Alistair Smith's 'accelerated learning cycle' (5) is an effective and popular way of managing the learning process in the delivery of content. It can be seen on the walls of hundreds of classrooms around the country.

In this section, the accelerated learning cycle is used as a model. There are seven stages to the cycle, in addition to a 'precursor' stage – creating a supportive learning environment – which is required for the other stages to be effective.

Model mapping can support the delivery of each stage. This section is divided up under the following headings, which reflect the stages in the accelerated learning cycle:

- **0** Creating a supportive learning environment
- **1** Connecting the learning
- **2** Big picture first
- **3** Outcomes
- **4** Input – VAK (visual, auditory, kinaesthetic)
- **5** Activity
- **6** Measuring progress and demonstrating understanding
- **7** Review for recall and retention

0 Creating a supportive learning environment

Mapping helps the teacher to create a supportive learning environment by affecting the three main aspects of the classroom:

- ◆ the physical environment
- ◆ the positive teacher
- ◆ the positive learner.

The physical environment

Displaying maps of work that have been completed, are under construction or are to be drawn, provides students with a way of pre-processing, processing or reviewing work. Model maps, because of their structure and the fact that each one is visually unique, can provide a visual reinforcement of learning that aids recall and understanding.

You can use model maps to show the personal goals and targets of your students alongside evidence of the achievement of these goals. Maps leave room for additional information to be added, so using model maps in this way enables you to work with the students to create a 'live' display that is constantly changing. You can discuss with students where best to place new items. Is there already a section where this can go? Do we need to add a new section? What questions does this new information help us to answer? These are all questions the students can consider when using the organisational principles of mapping to help create their displays.

"Would it help if you put up poster-sized graphic organisers, mind maps or webbing? Yes. It worked in 135 studies that examined the effects of pre-organisers where some form of previewing technique was used. Mapping … gives learners a way of conceptualising ideas, shaping thinking and understanding better what they know."

E. Jensen (6)

The positive teacher

Being able to model map often gives teachers a massive boost in personal confidence – having mapped out the topic, they are reassured of their own understanding of it, and they know they can really teach it (as opposed to simply disseminating information). By using model maps you can be sure that you know how to share your personal understanding and knowledge of anything with your students. You can also use this same tool in working with students to identify what they already know and to literally see their progress as they learn.

"A major benefit of mapping is that we can use this practical, visually orientated strategy within the context of any topic in the school curriculum."

Robert Fisher (1) (reproduced with the permission of Stanley Thornes Publishers Ltd, from Teaching Children to Learn by Robert Fisher, first published in 1995)

The positive learner

When the benefits that you as a teacher have gained from model mapping are taught to students, they can transform their learning experience. Once students know how they construct understanding and meaning – once they know how they learn – they are far more willing to engage in the learning process with you.

"… the learner must choose to learn meaningfully: that is, the learner must deliberately choose to relate new knowledge to knowledge the learner already knows in some non-trivial way."

Joseph Novak (3)

When we get beneath all the issues about processes and environment, the fact is that learning takes place in the learner. The ultimate aim of a teacher is to help students to engage – to enable them to be independent learners. Independent learners are able to take responsibility for their participation and for achieving desired learning outcomes. Having learners that can take full responsibility for their learning creates a whole new dynamic for classroom interactions between you and your students. Model mapping is a proven way to help you achieve this.

1 Connecting the learning

Model mapping provides a clear, visible link between what has gone before and what is to come. Teachers cannot be sure that any learning is taking place unless they know

what the students already know. If we do not start from where students are, it is not surprising that they do not connect to new information presented to them. Unless we connect the plug to the socket there is no point in trying to switch the light on.

If we connect to what learners already know the consequences are likely to be positive ones, including greater depth of understanding and recall. If we do not connect, then we increase the likelihood of negative consequences, including behavioural problems.

Using models of your thinking and creating maps with students also clarifies key vocabulary, categories and links that may occur in the learning to come. Unlike linear notes, there is room to add additional information as you and the students progress through the activities.

In all areas of education, teachers use model mapping to show the class how much they all already know about the topic to be taught. On the next page, a colleague working with a year 8 class in an Essex special school describes his experience of using model mapping as a way of connecting the learning.

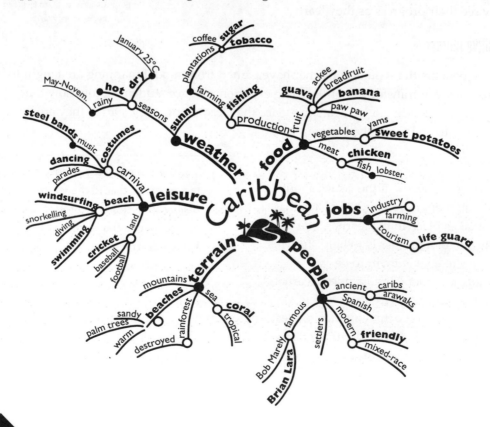

"It was immediately apparent to me that the class were suffering from 'death by worksheet'. I was told that they were due to start some Geography work on the Caribbean. I thought a good place to start, therefore, was to map what we as a class already knew about this part of the world – you could say I was 'connecting their learning'. I started by asking the class to think of one, three or five words that they associated with this region. As they fed back their words to me I started producing a map on a blackboard. It seemed to me that the students very quickly realised how I was organising the information into the different categories and started to think of additional words associated with those already on the board. Within minutes the blackboard had a map on it with branches covering landscape, weather, holidays, industry, food, and people. I was amazed at what they already knew given the perception I had of their limited life experiences …"

This teacher had never worked with this class of children before. By using model mapping, he was able to piece together a very clear picture (literally) of the students' current knowledge and understanding about the Caribbean. In doing so he also established a resource or baseline upon which he could build.

 "The brain makes many more connections when prior learning is activated; thus, learning, comprehension, and meaning increases. Many learners … under-perform because the new material seems irrelevant."

E. Jensen (6)

2 Big picture first

A model map can provide as big a picture as you need. Displaying a map of a lesson, or of a unit of work, or of a whole scheme of work gives your students an overview of work to be covered. As students become familiar with using maps, they are supported and become more adept at adding their own information.

All students benefit from knowing where they are going and how to get there.

 "One sees great things from the valley, only small things from the peak."

C. K. Chesterton

You can give students their own copies of 'big picture' maps before they start a lesson, unit or scheme. In doing so, you are giving them the box lid for the jigsaw that you will be piecing together with them. You can 'walk' through the branches of your model maps with your students, explaining how you made each of the connections. In doing this, you are making available to the students not only the product of your thinking (which all teachers do) but, most importantly, the process of your thinking. As a teacher, you already provide a role model for your students – now you can model your own thinking for them too. A colleague describes what happened when he started to do this in his Maths lessons: "I was amazed at the difference using maps in this way made to my classes. The very first time I put the map of the term's work onto overhead acetate students started asking questions. As I traced over the branches I explained to the class why I had organised the work in the way I had done. The class started questioning my logic, my thinking. They were saying things like 'What about such-and-such, sir – shouldn't that be included?' and 'Why have you put this here? Couldn't it go with that over there, sir?' It was incredible. The map provided them with a focus for asking me questions. For my part I knew exactly what they were asking questions about. Not only were they supported by the map in explaining their question they could also show me exactly where the problem or question arose from."

Model maps can transform the nature of teacher–student relationships in the classroom. By asking questions, students can tell you what they need to know – they can actually teach you how to teach.

3 Outcomes

Model maps give you a very easy and clear way of letting students know what the outcomes of their work will be. If you display a map for the current unit of work, you can make reference to the specific part of it that they will be working on. The students can see how the outcomes of the lesson fit in with the whole. Outcomes can be 'ticked off' or highlighted as they are achieved, either on class-based model maps or on individual ones. The physical presence of a map can encourage your students to take an interest in desired outcomes.

4 Input – VAK (visual, auditory, kinaesthetic)

As a teacher you are providing opportunities for the students in your class to see, hear and feel certain things. When you provide visual, auditory and kinaesthetic (VAK) input you are increasing the likelihood that your students will make a connection between a current stimulus and previous experience and understanding.

Other books look in detail at ways in which you can enrich learning by providing a variety of VAK input in your lessons (4, 5, 7, 8). This book, however, concentrates on the construction of meaning and understanding. Set out below are ways in which maps can be used as part of the delivery of visual, auditory and kinaesthetic input, though of course maps also play a more significant role in actually demonstrating the meaning-making process.

"We make sense out of the world through transforming our perceptions (what we see, hear, feel etc.) into concepts (words and ideas)."

Robert Fisher (1) (reproduced with the permission of Stanley Thornes Publishers Ltd, from Teaching Children to Learn by Robert Fisher, first published in 1995)

Visual input

A presentation of your thinking as a model map is the most visual form of input your students could receive.

Students are often subjected to what has been termed 'one-pass learning' – as the teacher delivers information orally, they have to grasp and retain it immediately; the teacher's spoken word, if not captured, is quickly lost. The sequencing of information in this kind of spoken communication is necessarily linear, which means students have to maintain constant attention to follow the 'story'; if that attention is broken, the students have no obvious means of picking up the thread again.

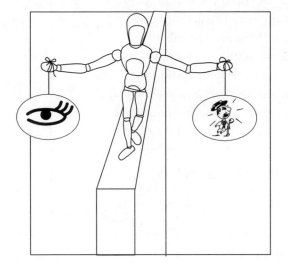

These problems are resolved with the use of model maps. Maps are static and allow the student the chance to assimilate and reflect on the information. Visual information, unlike the spoken word, is not structured by time. That is to say, what you said five minutes ago can be viewed, with a model map, at the same time as what you are saying right now. Students can review what has been said and place new information into a structure to give it meaning. The primary task of a student in receiving your delivery is to make sense of it – and she does this by referring it to past knowledge. When that knowledge is visible in front of her, the task is far more easily accomplished.

Auditory input

For most, teaching primarily involves speaking and listening. Explanation is at the heart of teaching. While it is subject to time, in the sense that one spoken idea has to follow another, speaking can also transcend time because the speaker can move readily from current information to past knowledge. To follow such jumps can be intellectually interesting and exciting, but it runs the risk of losing the listener. With the backup of a visual 'big picture' map, you need not limit the adventurous nature of your spoken delivery. Model maps can support such flights because everyone is able to see, literally, where it is you have gone in your speaking. Your jumps are made visible and therefore traceable, so that learners can literally 'see' what you are saying.

Kinaesthetic input — polebridging

Wim Wenger (9) originated the concept of 'polebridging', which involves talking through your thinking. When it is used in explaining a model map, it becomes a very powerful way of integrating kinaesthetic input into your teaching. For example, as you talk through your map with a class and explain the thinking behind its organisation, you can also physically 'walk' your finger along the branches. Your students can follow your thinking with their own fingers on their own maps as you demonstrate your explanation. The activity as a whole therefore appeals to students with any learning preference, visual, auditory or kinaesthetic: they can see the map, hear your explanation and move their hands. A powerful example of polebridging is given below in the section on 'Measuring progress and demonstrating understanding' (page 161).

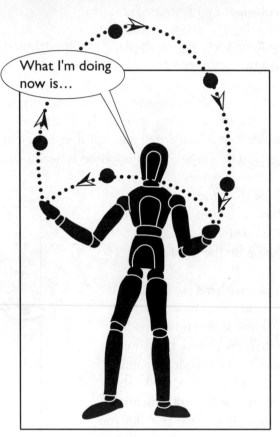

What I'm doing now is...

5 Activity

Model mapping can support individual, group and whole-class work, either as part of an activity, or after an activity. It cannot be used as a completely free-standing activity because you always need to be mapping *something*. Its real power is in providing the teacher with a means of measuring the level of students' understanding without having to rely exclusively on verbal or linear explanation.

"Maps furnish a bird's eye view that can reveal new connections, prompt new ideas."

S. Ostrander and L. Schroeder (10)

Active learning

Model mapping promotes active learning. It is worth making a distinction between physically active learning and cognitively active learning. Not all 'active learning' needs to be physical. Active learning, whether 'physical' or 'cognitive', is based on the learner taking a personal view of the information offered. She must 'retranslate' the information provided by the teacher or the text into her own individual understanding. This can often be accomplished by the learner changing textual information into a map or chart, or vice versa. It is this involvement with the meaning of the information that lies at the heart of active learning. Model mapping offers a highly effective and flexible way of engaging students. While it is possible to take traditional, linear notes in a fairly mindless way, it is impossible to construct a model map without being intellectually active and involved with the core concepts and details of the subject under study.

"We have found a greater willingness, especially in boys, to redo concept maps than to rewrite reports or themes."

J. D. Novak and D. B. Gowin (11)

Planning a talk, presentation or essay — making notes

Some students are able to select and organise information either into a plan or directly into a drafted piece of work. This is an incredible skill. We should not assume that all students can do it, and we must develop ways to help those who cannot if we are to prevent underachievement and its consequences.

You can help students with different levels of planning skill by differentiating the structure upon which the plan is to be based. Not all students are able to identify the main organising principles for an essay. It can be useful, therefore, to discuss the topic with the group and decide what the main branches of a model map of that topic might be. You could provide a template for students with these branches already present, to help structure their thinking. For some students, the main branches alone may be insufficient; they might need the sub-branches to be provided too in order to access the specific (less abstract) details and examples.

Below is an account given by a Secondary SENCO of the difference that model mapping made to Patrick, a student in a secondary comprehensive school.

"Patrick is in year 8. He has learning difficulties and is on stage 3 of assessment. Whilst staff did acknowledge that Patrick had some difficulties with learning, he presented himself primarily as a child with behavioural difficulties. Classwork, if attempted, was disorganised both in terms of its structure and its layout on the page. He displayed the classic survival behaviours of fight, flight, flock and freeze. When asked to produce a plan of a forthcoming piece of work he would often produce a blank sheet! I worked with his class for three one-hour sessions using model mapping photocopy masters. At the end of this, Patrick produced a model map on sport. He did this without prompting and when I asked him if I could have a copy he insisted on redrafting it neat for me."

Patrick's map is shown here. Look at the way he has organised his knowledge about sport. Examine the vocabulary he has used. Look at the spellings that he has attempted. The map illustrates the difference that model mapping can make to an individual who has had difficulty in organising his thoughts – both in terms of his ability to make sense of the information but also in the difference that it made to his feelings about himself as a learner.

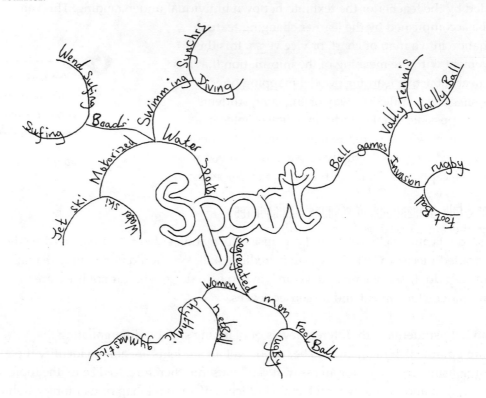

Taking notes

Taking notes is harder than making notes; that is to say, keeping a written record of someone's (usually oral) delivery of information as it happens is more difficult than organising and setting down information from your own experience or from existing written sources. Taking notes involves the creation of understanding and meaning from information that another person has organised – for example, from a lecture, lesson, video, TV programme or radio broadcast. Making notes, on the other hand, is based on the creation and categorisation of information to which the learner has had some prior exposure.

"… good learning typically goes with the systematic encoding of incoming material, integrating and relating it to what is already known."

A. D. Baddeley (12)

Using model maps as a way of taking notes is a powerful and effective learning tool. Linear note-taking is time-consuming, sometimes overwhelming and confusing, and does not necessarily involve any creation of meaning or demonstration of understanding; model maps, on the other hand, allow the learner to capture and make sense of the information without having to write down nearly so much. As the learner creates the map, he is able to see simultaneously the 'big picture' and the elements that make it up. This means that as the speaker proceeds, the learner is able quickly to identify relationships (similarities and differences) between each piece of new information and what has gone before, and fit new links and branches into the existing structure of his map. The structure of the map also helps the learner to predict what information is to follow, to a certain extent. The learner is creating his own model of understanding as he goes along.

Note-taking using model mapping does take some practice. It is useful at first, therefore, to suggest suitable keywords (which are the main organising concepts of the topic) to the students before asking them to take notes. Alternatively, you could provide them with a 'skeleton' model mapping structure on paper, to help them practise taking notes in this way.

6 Measuring progress and demonstrating understanding

If you use a model map to help you complete a journey not only does it confirm that you have arrived at your intended destination, it also shows you where you are on the way.

If you, as the teacher, provide students with model map overviews of the schemes, units and individual elements of their study, they can see where they are and where they are going. By asking students to produce their own model map at various stages of a topic's delivery, you can see how much they have added to their understanding. The same map can usually be used at each stage because students are adding new key information to existing levels of understanding. Give out an A3 sheet of paper at the beginning of a topic and ask pupils to build a picture of their understanding as they go though the work. In this way, you are measuring progress; they are demonstrating their learning.

"The ability to express an idea is well nigh as important as the idea itself."

Bernard Barush, US Statesman

There is a tendency for teachers to view model mapping simply as a good tool for revision and planning. But maps are perhaps most powerful when used by the learner to explain or demonstrate her learning. The process of producing a model map is at least as valuable as the product itself.

An A level Psychology teacher describes her experience of mapping: "I used a model mapping photocopy master pack and subject-specific content to teach my A level students how to map. As it turned out, this provided a useful revision exercise – it was not time away from our work at all in the end. After the initial tuition, I had a much clearer idea about the levels my students were working at. I then put the students into groups of three or four and asked them to collaboratively produce a model map relating to a particular area of their study that I gave each group. After a brief period (my students were not comfortable or familiar with working collaboratively on such a focused task in this way), I watched amazed as they engaged in very deep dialogue about the work we had covered in psychology. A colleague popped in and stayed … equally amazed. We were witnessing students discussing how they were shaping and organising their thinking. By model mapping, they were producing a model of their understanding … I can see what is missing in terms of my explanation, planning and delivery."

Information is stored in the long-term memory when understanding and meaning is gained. The best way to see if you understand something is to explain it to someone else. If you cannot, then the chances are you did not fully understand it in the first place. The same applies to your students. Model maps are a way of allowing students to demonstrate their understanding without the pressure and perhaps anxiety associated with producing linear notes (essays) or oral explanations. From your own perspective as a teacher, not only can marking time be greatly reduced by using model maps, but you gain a clearer understanding of the levels at which your students are working.

"Understanding is a precious commodity – the holy grail of the classroom, to be planned, nurtured and cherished – because without it, there can be no genuine learning."

Mike Hughes (8)

"We do not, even after careful explanation and examples, know whether a concept has been assimilated into a child's wider knowledge of the world until we ask the child to represent and share what they know."

Robert Fisher (1) (reproduced with the permission of Stanley Thornes Publishers Ltd, from Teaching Children to Learn *by Robert Fisher, first published in 1995)*

So, a powerful way of getting students to demonstrate their understanding is to ask them to produce a model map of the work covered. You could ask them to model map the lesson, or if you have finished a unit of work, you could ask them to map the whole unit.

Case studies

 Having used model mapping as a planning tool, a group of Business Studies students demonstrated their understanding of a particular unit of work to their peers. The students explained their maps (by 'walking and talking' them through) using overhead acetates. As they went through the branches of their maps, they added detail and explained their thinking, which was represented as a model in front of them.

Where the students reached a section of the map that they were unable to explain to the class, it became apparent that they had not fully grasped or understood this particular part of it. The map provided the means to direct and focus discussion. It led to clarification of the point where a breakdown of understanding had occurred.

Because the focus of the discussion was the model, and not the student, the breakdown of understanding was not viewed as 'bad' or 'dramatic' in any sense. Indeed, the teacher commented on how the model map helped the students to support each other. The class asked questions when they did not understand any part of the map that was being explained. Unlike most scenarios where a student utters those immortal words "I don't understand", the students here were able to say exactly where their lack of understanding lay. So the map not only supported the 'teacher' (in this case a student) in explaining the topic, it also acted as a physical support for the students around which to shape their questions. (One example of the students' maps is shown on page 151.)

"... have them [students] read their map as a story one or two days after it was completed. Students who construct good maps will show remarkable fidelity in reproducing the meaning of text, even though they have not memorised the text."

J. D. Novak and D. B. Gowin (11)

 You can also use mapping as a means of continuously monitoring students' understanding. Let us return to the year 8 classroom where the teacher has used mapping to establish what the students already know about the Caribbean (see page 154). The teacher continues:

"I left the map [showing the children's current knowledge of the Caribbean] on the board. We then looked at and discussed a series of photographs on the Caribbean theme from a resource pack. What I noticed was how the students kept looking from the map to the photographs. As our discussion went on we started working out where on the map to place any additional vocabulary, pictures or ideas emerging from our discussion. The students did not know how to map but the way the map was organised seemed to support their interest. This time the students wrote the words, or drew simple icons or pictures on the board as we went along and before long the blackboard was packed with an in-depth summary of our work.

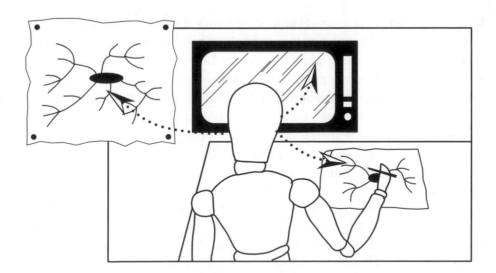

"I decided to see how much of the information on the board they could talk about. I was amazed at how they were constantly looking at the board as if seeking clarification or maybe it was vocabulary. I think that the blackboard gave the students confidence and the freedom to concentrate on the task at hand. They did not have to make a conscious effort to remember what we had covered thus far – the blackboard did this for them.

"We then watched a 20-minute video. Before we started watching, I asked the students to draw the main branches from our map onto a blank sheet of A4 paper and I asked them to add words to the branches as we watched the video. As the video progressed my attention was taken away from the screen completely by what I was witnessing the students do. These students (remember they had quite complex levels of general learning difficulties) were now cross-referencing three different areas. They were watching the video, looking at our map and then recording any new information on their sheets."

3 In *Accelerated Learning in the Primary School* (4) a year 6 teacher outlines a similar experience to that described above: "One of the most remarkable moments of my career was when I was teaching photosynthesis with my year 6 class. We memory-mapped our understanding on the whiteboard. Each child came up and took a pen, adding a keyword or symbol to the memory map and talked through his or her thoughts aloud. Our memory map grew and grew, as we saw the connections between photosynthesis and the work we had done on the rain forests, the ozone layer, respiration, habitats, the human body, smoking, digestion, the plants, the elements, the periodic table, and so on. By the end of the afternoon we had a memory map that represented to us the wonder of the universe … Connections had been made that had never occurred to me. It was so exciting, a time of revelation. The power of memory mapping became so clear to me. I could see where other connections could be made for future learning, and that nothing needed to be learned in isolation."

4 Here two primary practitioners outline how they use maps to measure understanding and learning in their school: "When the topic comes to an end, we then reflect on what the children have learnt, how they've developed their knowledge. The examples given by the children in year 4 and year 2 show how they can use the initial concept map to reflect upon and add new detail to. It is a powerful learning tool, and a great physical piece of evidence to show children where they started with their learning and compare it to what they know later. We envisage that all children will have concept mapping books that they take with them throughout the school, adding new learning details and reflecting a lot more on what they have learnt."

7 Review for recall and retention

Model mapping provides a wealth of 'hooks' to aid recall – keywords, categories, images, symbols, colour and dimension all add up to make each model map unique. A section of linear text can be unique but it does not look unique, and so it is very much more difficult to recall the information it contains.

The way that maps have been used during the delivery of a lesson or topic will affect how they can be used for review and recall. If students have been drawing their own maps to demonstrate understanding of various units of work you could ask them to 'walk and talk' through (explain) their maps to a partner, group or the class. Ask them to explain the map to their parents for homework. You could set an assignment asking them to put together a number of maps into a combined, poster-sized map.

If students have not been using maps as part of their work until now, you could set up an end-of-topic review activity in which each student (or group of students) has to produce a map of the topic for display or presentation to the rest of the class.

"Memory is primarily a process of making links, connections and associations between new information and existing patterns of knowledge. Memory depends in large part on keywords and key concepts that, when properly remembered, are transferred from short-term memory to long-term memory. It is through the linking of information to existing patterns of knowledge that we create new forms of understanding. If we cannot identify keywords and concepts, and have not created patterns of understanding then our understanding and our meaning become fragmentary – we have not grasped things, we have not created an effective map."

Robert Fisher (1) (reproduced with the permission of Stanley Thornes Publishers Ltd, from Teaching Children to Learn *by Robert Fisher, first published in 1995)*

For older students, producing model maps as part of an independent revision schedule is an obvious way of using maps for review and recall. A student that has several relevant maps in mind, which he can 'dump' down onto paper as soon as he gets into the examination hall, is at an advantage over other students still relying on linear notes, since linear notes are so much harder to recall in full and so much more time-consuming to reproduce.

You can produce maps for students, to summarise key topics for revision. Use A3 paper and leave lots of white space on the map so that the students can add their own branches and comments. In this way, you are sharing and making visible your expertise and understanding, but students are able to add to it easily to make it their own.

"They [maps] give an extra edge when you need to recall your data. A map lights up in the mind more quickly than a list. Why? Because it's a picture. Anything you can visualise, you will learn faster and remember longer."

S. Ostrander and L. Schroeder (10)

"The allure of being able to summarise all the areas for revision on one side of A3 is immense. Students will happily stay on task producing maps and discussing texts in detail and take home their condensed revision aid. Last year I used model mapping with my year 11 students. Most students in the class achieved one grade higher than I had predicted at Christmas. The students said they found it easier to revise from and that they had pinned their maps up in their bedrooms to look at regularly."

Val Hill, Head of English, and Teaching and Learning, Stewards School, Harlow

Review

chapter six

CREDITS

1 Consider your current practice in the classroom. Use Alistair Smith's accelerated learning cycle to help you identify what you consider to be your strengths and weaknesses in managing the learning process. Use this chapter to help you identify ways that model mapping could help you to develop your skills in these areas.

2 Map the ways that you will use model maps as part of your classroom practice. Set out when you will do it and with which classes. Tell someone you are going to do it. Ask them to ask you how it went.

3 Visualise yourself using model maps in each of the areas you have decided. Visualise the difference that maps will make.

MAPWISE — accelerated learning through visible thinking

Cleverness and internal maps

understanding how we understand

MAPWISE — accelerated learning through visible thinking

Chapter 7

Cleverness and internal maps

understanding how we understand

COMING SOON!

1 What clever people do that makes us think they are clever.
2 How we can model 'cleverness'.
3 How to make this 'cleverness' available to others.
4 What cognitive psychologists mean when they talk about personal schemas.
5 Why knowing about personal schemas has extremely important implications for teaching and learning.
6 How understanding and revealing personal schemas aid learning.

"The issue of intelligence is of course a contentious one. As a neuroscientist, my definition would hark back to Latin, in terms of understanding – the more one can associate an issue with other things, 'see it' in terms of prior facts, processes, values etc., the more perhaps that one can be said to have understood the issue. If so, then 'true' intelligence, would be the ability to relate any process, person, fact or object in turn to prior experiences."

Professor Susan Greenfield (1)

MAPWISE — accelerated learning through visible thinking

There is a bird in the Grand Canyon in the United States called the nutcracker. It eats a particular nut that is only ripe for three weeks each year. During these three weeks the nutcracker is to be seen flying about gathering and burying its nuts ready for the remaining 49 weeks. During this intensive three week spell, the nutcracker buries between 25,000 and 30,000 nuts over a radius of 80 square miles. It remembers where it has placed the nuts by breaking the landscape down into areas (visual categories) and these areas into sub-categories. Even snowfall does not prevent the nutcracker from finding more than 90% of the nuts it has buried! How do we know this? A very clever little bird told us!

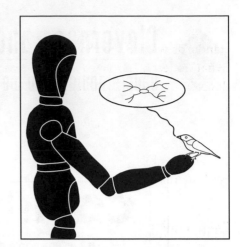

"Developing thinking skills is supported by theories of cognition which see learners as active creators of their knowledge and frameworks of interpretation. Learning is about searching out meaning and imposing structure."

Carol McGuiness (2)

This chapter is divided up into the following sections:

- ◆ Intellectual capital
- ◆ Being clever
- ◆ Distinguishing cleverness
- ◆ Giving it away
- ◆ Putting cleverness into schools.

◆ Intellectual capital

We are living in the age of information where intelligence is prized above everything else. Today, companies are not judged by concrete assets such as premises and machinery, but rather by their intellectual capital.

Nations have responded to this change in focus by committing themselves to raising educational standards. They are very clear that the economic health of their countries will be directly related to the intellectual growth of their workers and potential workers (the school population). New curricula and rigorous inspection schemes have had varying effects in identifying, changing or removing those schools which under-achieve. Their sophistication and impact reflect the scale in which they are operating.

The issue of raising personal intellectual activity, however, requires an altogether different approach. Recent government moves to encourage the use of accelerated learning in UK schools, and the inclusion of thinking skills into subject teaching in the new National Curriculum, are promising. They suggest that the government has realised that in order to raise standards we need to move away from the debate about 'what' to teach and learn, and move on to examine and develop 'how' best to achieve this.

How can we all be as clever as the nutcracker? Is it possible to identify what the 'clever ones' do and make this process available to the majority? In this chapter we see how this is possible.

"Most intelligent people appreciate that information is [now] a much bigger part of our lives. The problem is that we are still overlaying more and more information on top of old ways of processing it."

John Sculley, former Chairman of Apple Computers Inc (in 3)

◆ Being clever

Can you remember individuals from your own school days who won all the academic accolades? We admire their results and are left feeling that they have something special we just don't have – they seem to have some sort of secret that they won't share. It could be that clever people have certain beliefs about their own cleverness, which mean they keep their 'secret' to themselves:

1 First, the very features of their cleverness are probably not well known to them. They are unaware of what it is that distinguishes them from their fellow human beings. Clearly, they are aware of the effect their thinking has on others – admiration, validation, envy, aggression even. What is not apparent is how the product (story, report, essay, exam result) was achieved. In other words, how did the 'cleverness' work? They know that they are clever but do not know how they are clever.

2 Second, clever people may have an almost superstitious belief that if the workings of 'cleverness' were known to them, the magic would cease. Perhaps they believe that 'cleverness' is a kind of mystical gift bestowed on special people. Because they are unaware of the workings of their cleverness, they sanctify its mystery by not investigating it.

3 Third, perhaps there is a slightly selfish attitude about their gift of cleverness. Being so prized, it is coveted. To give it away, in the sense of sharing how the product of their thinking was constructed, would be to lessen its worth.

We do not see what clever people do, only the final result. Simply getting to see the final product of clever thinking certainly impresses with its brilliance, but it is not empowering. What if we could make intelligence public and have it in front of us, so we could have a good look at it? What would we see that clever people actually do? Let us try to demystify cleverness and to democratise it – to 'give it away'.

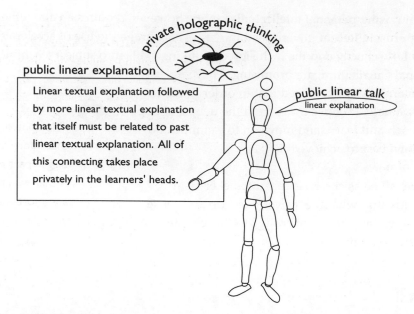

Even if he did not hold the limiting beliefs listed above, a clever person would not find it easy to explain how his cleverness works. There seems to be no ready model available that makes the invisible visible, the abstract concrete, the ephemeral permanent, the fleeting static or the private public. But this is exactly what we need to do in order to 'capture' the private nature of cleverness.

◆ Distinguishing cleverness

There have been many ways of looking at intelligence. These perspectives shape our view of intelligence and offer some insights into the working of cleverness itself. On the whole, these perspectives, or models, tell us how cleverness manifests itself in actions, attitudes, attributes and strategies. Howard Gardner's multiple intelligences model, for example, sets out eight areas of intelligence that we can identify in students in school. This is a useful model. It supports us in providing a greater variety of experiences for students, and shows where we are perhaps being too narrow in our approach. However, it does not tell us what happens when this intelligence is working – it doesn't explain 'how they did it'.

"Every map takes the limits of his own field of vision for the limits of the world."

Arthur Schopenhaur, nineteenth century philosopher

Models of intelligence do not, therefore, offer any great lever into knowing how clever people are clever. For that we need another distinction.

We know that we receive information through our senses. But how exactly do we transform our sense impressions into coherent views of the world? What mechanisms are there that allow for the meaningful absorption of new information? How do we know what we know?

"Neuroscience has discovered a great deal about neurons and synapses, but not nearly enough to guide educational practice. Currently, the span between brain and learning cannot support much of a load. Too many people marching in step across it could be dangerous. If we are looking for a basic science to help guide educational practice and policy, cognitive psychology is a much better bet."

J. T. Bruer (4)

This is where cognitive psychologists tell us more than neuroscientists. The last ten years have produced 95% of our understanding of how the brain learns and this better understanding has led teachers to be more skilful in promoting positive states for learning. It has not, however, added to our understanding of how our minds are constructed.

"Mental models are the images, assumptions, and stories which we carry in our minds of ourselves, other people, institutions, and every aspect of the world. Like a pane of glass framing and subtly distorting our vision, mental models determine what we see."

P. Senge (5)

By 'mind', we mean the fabric of meaning developed in each individual that constitutes a world view; a consciousness even. We could say that our minds are the shape, or collection of shapes, arrived at by making sense of our experiences. As Professor Susan Greenfield (1) puts it, "… throughout life the brain will be in constant dialogue with the environment as one interprets and reinforces experiences in the light of what has gone before. It is this personalisation of the brain that is inextricable from memories, that for me is the best biological definition of a 'mind'."

The technical term for this sense of shape is 'schema'. Schema is a term well known to students of psychology, while in the business world people refer to 'mental models'. The use of these terms is normally restricted to these domains.

Mental models or schemas are central factors in understanding, thinking and learning – factors that affect all of us, all our lives. When you try to solve a practical problem, a personal difficulty or a logistical crisis in your mind, by the end of the thought process you have worked out a way of understanding it; of gathering, collecting and organising your thoughts so that the problem makes sense. The organisation of your thinking is a schema. Even if you can't make sense of the problem, the thought that says 'I can't make sense of it' is a schema too.

"The only real voyage of discovery consists not in seeking new landscapes but in having new eyes."

Marcel Proust

Daniel Goleman (6) describes schemas as "The packets that organise information and make sense of experience". They "embody the rules and categories that order raw experience into coherent meaning".

"We are all natural model builders."

P. Senge (5)

If you think about it long enough, it becomes apparent that all knowledge and experience is packaged in schemas. "Schemas are the ghost in the machine, the intelligence that guides information as it flows through the mind" (6). Humans go on creating schemas all their lives, to deal with minute details and vast domains, from concrete bodily experiences to abstract feelings. As Rumelhart (8), a cognitive psychologist, explains schemas capture and organise everything: "Schemas can represent knowledge at all levels – from ideologies and cultural truths to knowledge about what constitutes an appropriate sentence in our language to knowledge about the meaning of a particular word to knowledge about what patterns of [sounds] are associated with what letters of the alphabet."

"Man looks at his world through transparent patterns or templates which he creates and then attempts to fit over the realities of which the world is composed. The fit is not always very good. Yet without such patterns the world appears to be such an undifferentiated homogeneity that man is unable to make any sense out of it. Even a poor fit is more helpful to him than nothing at all."

George A. Kelly (7)

Once we have captured our interpretations of our experiences in schemas, we can refer to them, compare them and organise them. In this way, we can reason about them. This is why schemas are the key to bringing the private nature of cleverness into a public forum.

"Mental Models are very important, very powerful and very individual. They are expressions of how we see the world, of our assumptions, of our biases, of our beliefs … usually, however, they are not explored explicitly."

D. Sherwood (9)

We know from recent research into schemas that they have 'shape' and that they capture the essence of concepts, events and experience. But how are schemas created? The way this happens is described by cognitive psychologist, Marshall (10), who tells us that: "A schema is a vehicle of memory, allowing organisation of an individual's similar experiences in such a way that the individual:

[1] can easily recognise additional experiences that are also similar, discriminating between these and ones that are dissimilar

[2] can access a generic framework that contains the essential elements of all these similar experiences, including verbal and non-verbal components

[3] can draw inferences, make estimates, create goals and develop plans using the framework, and

[4] can utilise skills, procedures or rules as needed when faced with a problem for which this particular framework is relevant."

Put simply, the creation of schemas takes place through organisation. The world and the individual interact perpetually. The interactions are in themselves meaningless; things just happen, and the individual adds meaning to them. The meaning resides in the meaning-maker, not in the event.

Ian recalls an example to illustrate the location of meaning: "When I talk about schemas I often refer to an advertisement that ran on television several years ago. In the opening shot, we see a youth running towards an old man. The meaning I attached to this was that the old man was about to be attacked. The next shot panned out and I saw a pallet full of bricks about to fall on the old man. I then attached a new meaning – that rather than putting the man's life at risk the youth was actually trying to save it. The advert made me think about how often I get 'stuck' with an interpretation."

"We don't see things as they are, we see things as we are."

Anais Nin

"There is nothing good or bad but thinking makes it so."

Hamlet

As Ian's story illustrates, it is through the creation of schemas that we create our experience of our lives.

"Experience is made up of the successive construing of events. It is not constituted merely by the succession of events themselves."

George A. Kelly (7)

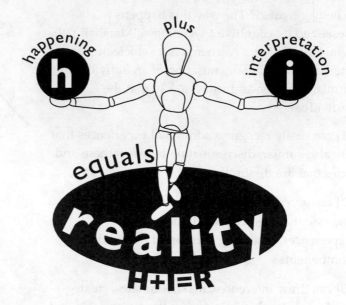

It is in human nature to create meaning from experience, and indeed it is probably essential for independent survival. We create meaning by organising the 'labels' that we attach to our experiences. It has been shown (11) that infants of three and four months can organise and conceptualise their experiences, even though they don't yet have language skills, and even though almost every experience in their young lives is a new one. So, we start very early, and continue to organise the meanings into ever more complex structures throughout our lives. These collections of meanings themselves create higher order meanings. This grasping for meaning is not passive but active – it is the way we understand (12).

"Hierarchical categories are important as means by which to organise expectations and regulate behaviour in the light of them."

James Britton (13)

Structures of meaning are built through hierarchical organisation, as shown in the illustration on the opposite page (from Goleman (6)). This is a traditional way of representing classification graphically. Goleman does not suggest that we consciously construct these diagrams in visual format in our heads. The diagram is not supposed to be a direct representation of thinking. It is a model or analogy of thinking.

So, all our thinking is structured along the same hierarchical lines as those used to describe schemas. We create categories of information, organised into hierarchies, and forge novel links between them based on each new experience.

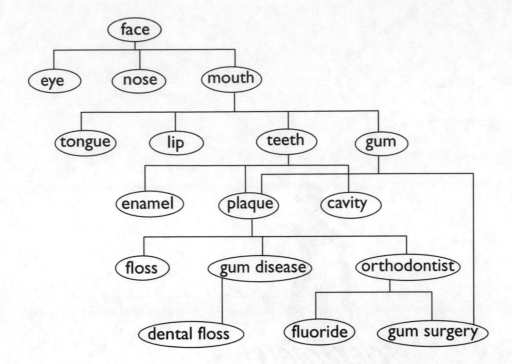

Clever people do exactly the same, but in more elaborate ways, making many more links and cross-connections between schemas. This allows them to:

◆ assimilate a great deal of information

◆ see connections between categories, and identify characteristics that either include or exclude items from categories

◆ switch focus quickly from overarching concept to peripheral detail

◆ recognise positions along the hierarchy of categories

◆ refashion the principles of the categorisation in order, to create a different arrangement or 'big picture'

◆ create new ideas and possibilities by seeing original relationships between categories

◆ store this architecture in a retrievable form.

This theory is supported by studies looking at the complexities of people's maps of ideas and understanding. Marshall (10) has found that "the more connections an individual makes at this level, the greater the understanding on the part of that individual." Novak (15) has recognised, in relation to concept mapping, that the more cross-connections are made the better the grasp on the subject. These cross-connections are not always obvious, and require a great deal of creativity to see them. They depend on the basic structure being in place in order to see beyond and across the fundamental organisation of content.

"The mind, we are convinced, selectively builds purposive models – paradigms – of events, using these to govern and increase its purchase on experience."

G. A. Woditsch (14)

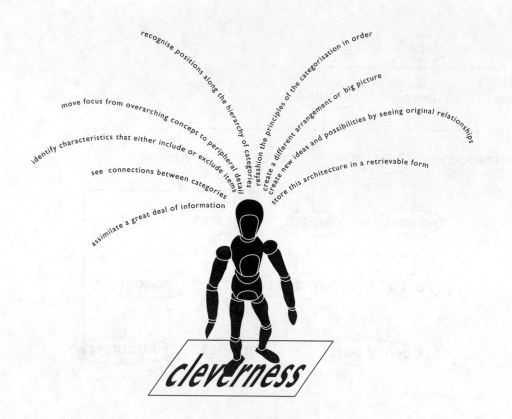

When used as models, visual maps – because their structure is dependent on the same hierarchical organisation of information upon which our thinking is based – offer a very powerful means of making private thinking public; of turning rapid decisions into static trails; of transforming abstractions to graspable graphics. Model maps represent thinking in a visible way. They are the vehicle for sharing cleverness.

"[An expert's] artistry is evident in his selective management of large amounts of information."

Donald Schon (16)

◆ Giving it away

There are now many attempts to capture and share others' intelligence or 'cleverness'. In a review of studies of novices learning from experts, Marshall (10) explains the attempts to catch private thinking: "For the most part, this new methodology [concept mapping] shifts attention away from the end product of reasoning and focuses instead on early and intermediate steps, which are usually unobservable. To tap into these unobserved processes, researchers ask their subjects to describe in detail their mental reasoning as they solve problems."

Academics have spent decades studying how professionals pass on their expertise. However, asking people to commentate on their thinking processes while they are taking place is problematic. Research into this area (17) has found that subjects were considerably hampered by this demand: "Verbalisation may cause such a ruckus in the front of one's mind that one is unable to attend to the new approaches that may be emerging in the back of one's mind."

This problem is acknowledged by management guru Paul Miller (18). Perhaps without realising quite how close he was to finding the way to achieve an answer to the problem, he notices that: "Soft knowledge … is difficult and at times impossible to access … You need a map to get to any destination – unless you have been to the place before. The information can come directly from the map, from someone else who has a map, or someone who has it 'in their head'".

A map of course makes this thinking public, static, graspable. These three qualities make one further benefit possible – shared explanation.

"Cogn... one wa... try to m..ke visible a conceptual structure, not simply to see what it is, but to process it, to challenge it and help enlarge it."

Robert Fisher (20) (reproduced with the permission of Stanley Thornes Publishers Ltd, from Teaching Children to Learn *by Robert Fisher, first published in 1995)*

◆ Putting cleverness into schools

"When educators realise that each one of us has our own 'model of the world', and this model is the reality as each of us perceives it, what a difference in education there will be! To be sure, there will not only be research into how an individual acquires these specific models, but more importantly, attention will be paid to meeting individuals at their models of the world. Increased rapport and subsequent effective communication would be the natural outcomes. Society would gain from the individual nature of each person's viewpoint. Schooling itself would change."

C. Van Nagel, E. J. Reese, M. Reese, R. Siudzinski (19)

Perhaps, then, what we mean by 'being clever' is no more than the combination of the apparently opposite skills of organisation and creativity. We can see that they are totally dependent on each other. Novel connections cannot be made until the basic structure is laid down. The organisation of content allows for this creative perspective. Without the content being hierarchically classified, there would be no patterns to discern.
In education, we have adopted the notion of left- and right-brain functions enthusiastically. The neuroscientists who make these discoveries are frustrated by the misleading popularisation of their discoveries and their inappropriate adoption by educators.

The lists of hemispheric faculties do often obscure more basic distinctions. Particular skills may indeed have particular locations in the brain, but we need to ask ourselves whether this information has any real significance. In other words, is this information merely interesting rather than empowering? Surely it is more useful to be able to recognise the relationships between creativity and organisation and between wholeness and parts.

"Remember that the elements of thoughts are constructs, shaped by the mind ... When better constructs arise in the mind, it is because the mind has fashioned them; not because some new, till-then-dormant insight was genetically triggered."

G. A. Woditsch (14)

The use of model maps encourages the use of both organisational and creative faculties. Maps demand the user to organise and they tease the user to be creative. They demonstrate the thinking behind the product; the 'ghost in the machine' is revealed. Cleverness is demystified and made evident. A model of what was internal – 'in the head' – has come out into the open. The abstract and private nature of schemas is transformed, through model maps, into the concrete and public. Blinding speed of thought has been captured in time, freeze-framed – a whole perspective has been captured and pictured. Now, we have the means of modelling cleverness.

If you wanted to learn a new activity such as golf, you might watch golf on the television, and soon after you might buy a book about golf techniques. This would start you using the language of golf. About the same time, you would probably start to buy a few golf clubs and try them out. Your participation at a golf club would give you contact with other golfers, both novice and expert. From both you would receive feedback on your technique. At this time, you might also pay for professional coaching. All these activities would, in their different ways, provide instruction on developing your golfing skills. The instruction would be related to the visible actions that constitute golfing – people are able to see what you're doing, and feed back accordingly.

If you were to learn any other skill, the same sort of learning process could take place, but with thinking, learning and understanding there is no obvious parallel. With the pervasive use of model maps, however, we can move closer to the golfing analogy in which the learner can benefit from continual and instant feedback from those around her.

If a whole school were to adopt model mapping, it might be possible to duplicate the culture of obvious and natural learning that takes place outside of school. Students could watch their expert peers 'doing' thinking, 'walking' through their model maps. School policies, student materials and posters could demonstrate constantly the mechanics of mapping, as well as the principles of the subject content. Different subjects would offer different terrains in which to practise mapping skills. Teachers and students could be coaches for personal instruction. 'Star mappers' could hold clinics to demonstrate and explain their skills; master classes could develop additional refinements. Talk among students and staff would be explicit, making direct references to the public, shared model maps. Feedback would be ongoing assessment for learning rather than stressful assessment of learning. Cleverness would be a graspable, shared commodity, out in the open and available to all.

Review
chapter seven

CREDITS

1 Think of someone you have always considered to be 'cleverer' than yourself. What insight into her cleverness has this chapter given you?
What questions might you now ask this person to understand better how she knows what she knows?

2 What personal schemas or models can you now identify for different areas of your life? What schemas do you think other people that you know or work with have? How might model mapping
  ■ help you share with others how you think?
  ■ help you solve or identify differences of opinion?

3 What possibilities can you see for your school from having read this chapter? How could model mapping be used to
  ■ access and share 'cleverness'?
  ■ support students with personal difficulties?
  ■ align all teaching staff on school aims?

Gallery of maps

The following pages show some examples of model maps produced by the authors, by classroom teachers and by students, for a variety of purpose.

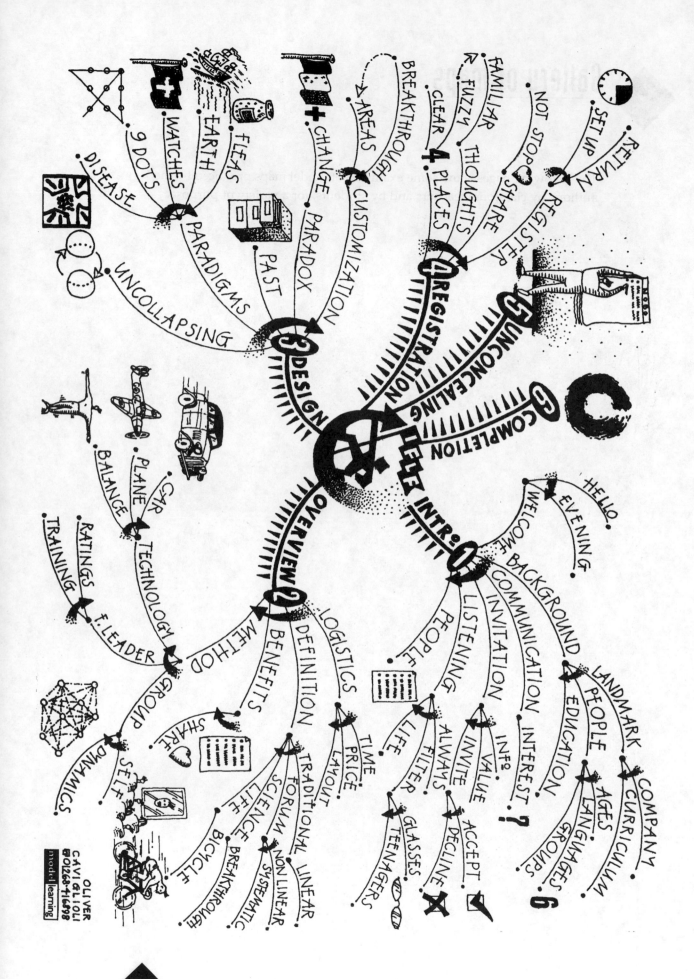

MAPWISE — accelerated learning through visible thinking

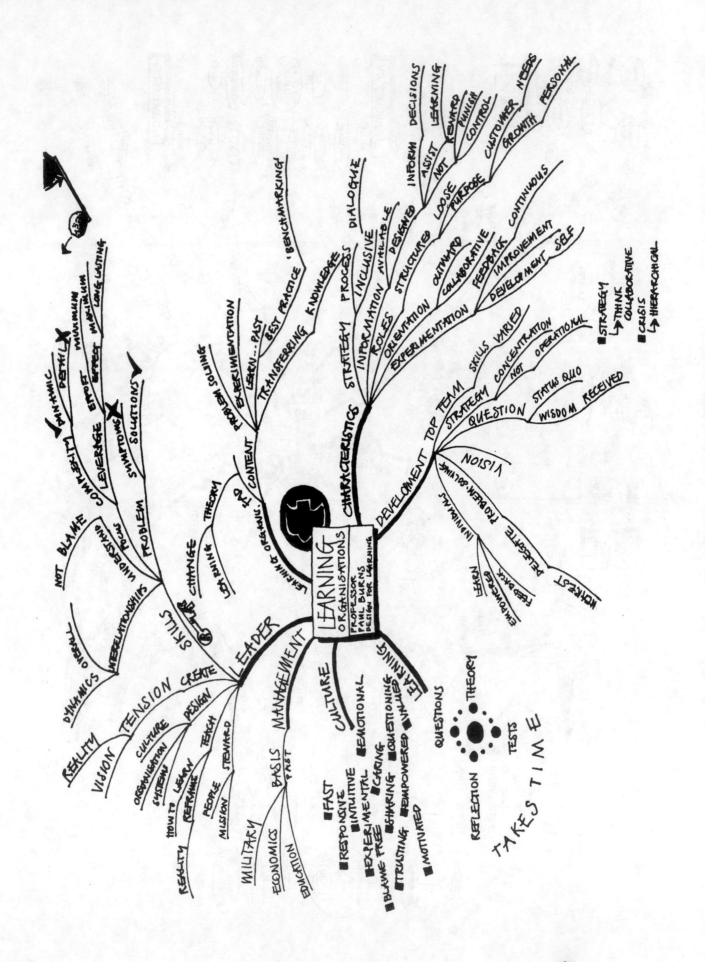

MAPWISE — accelerated learning through visible thinking

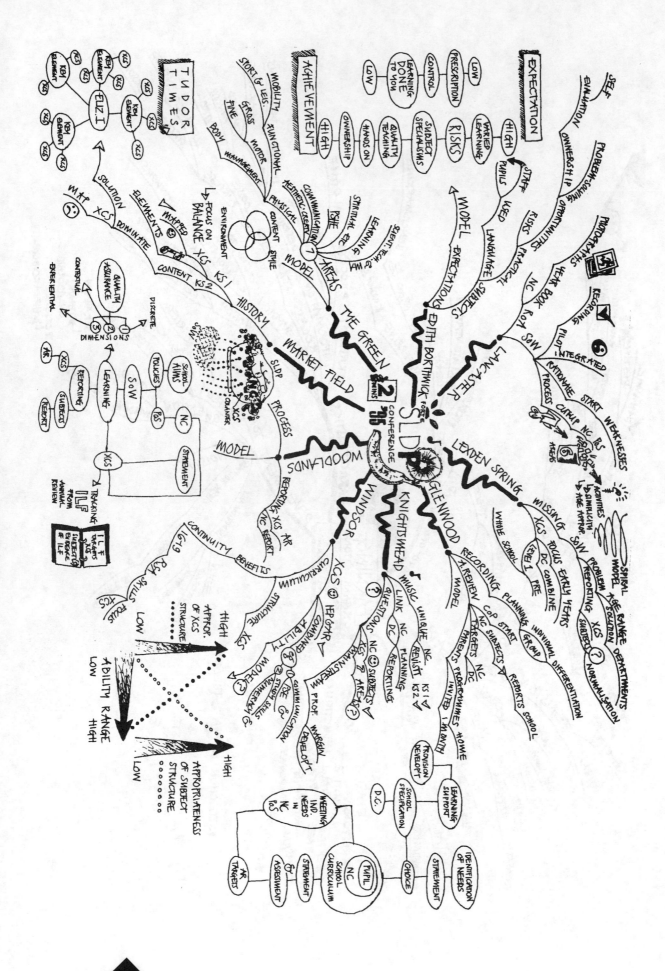

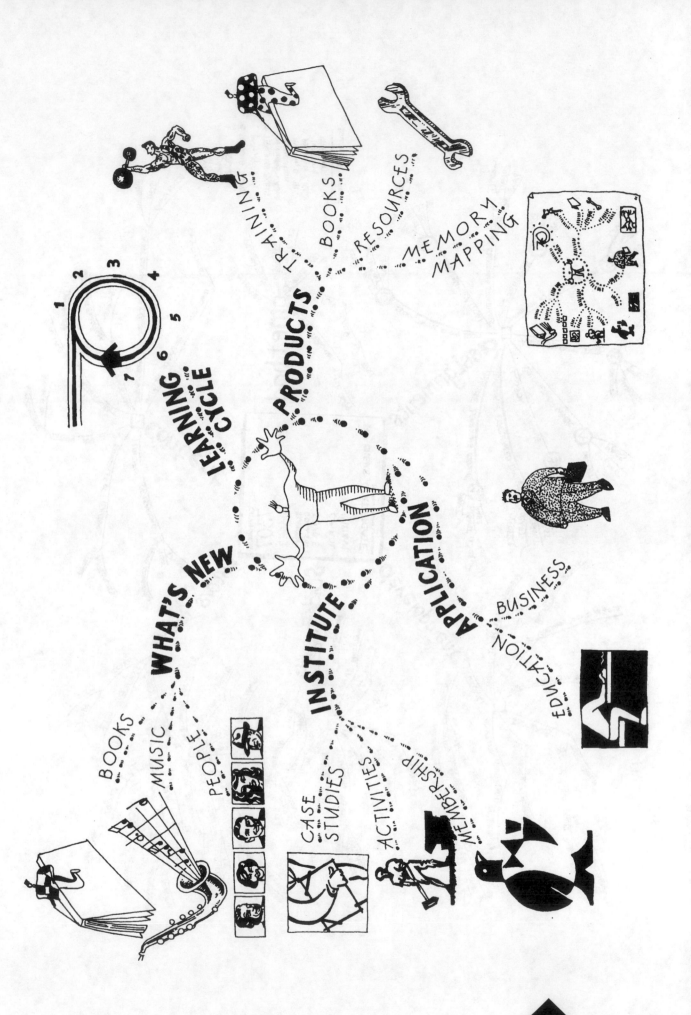

MAPWISE — accelerated learning through visible thinking

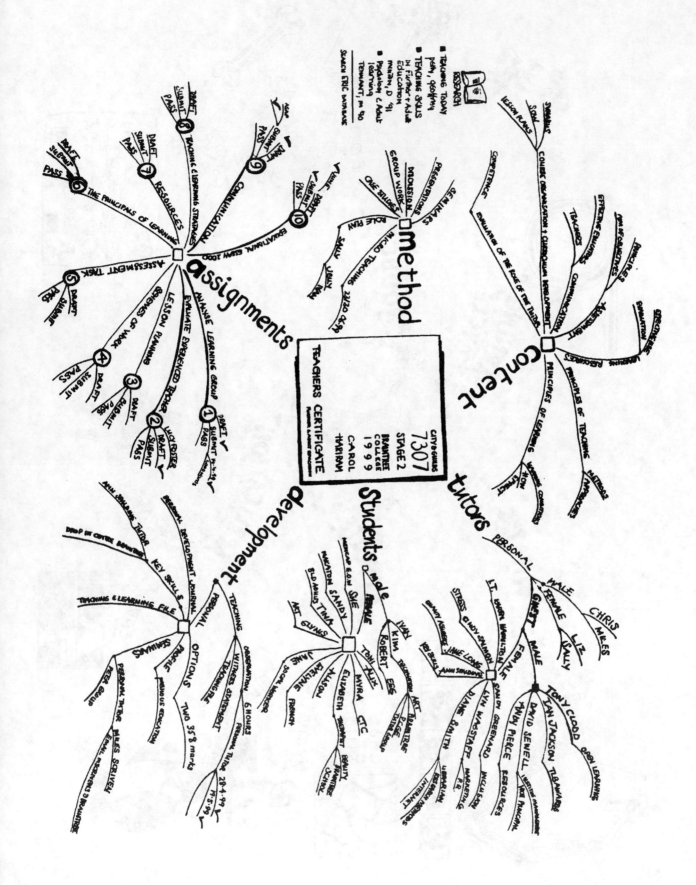

MAPWISE — accelerated learning through visible thinking

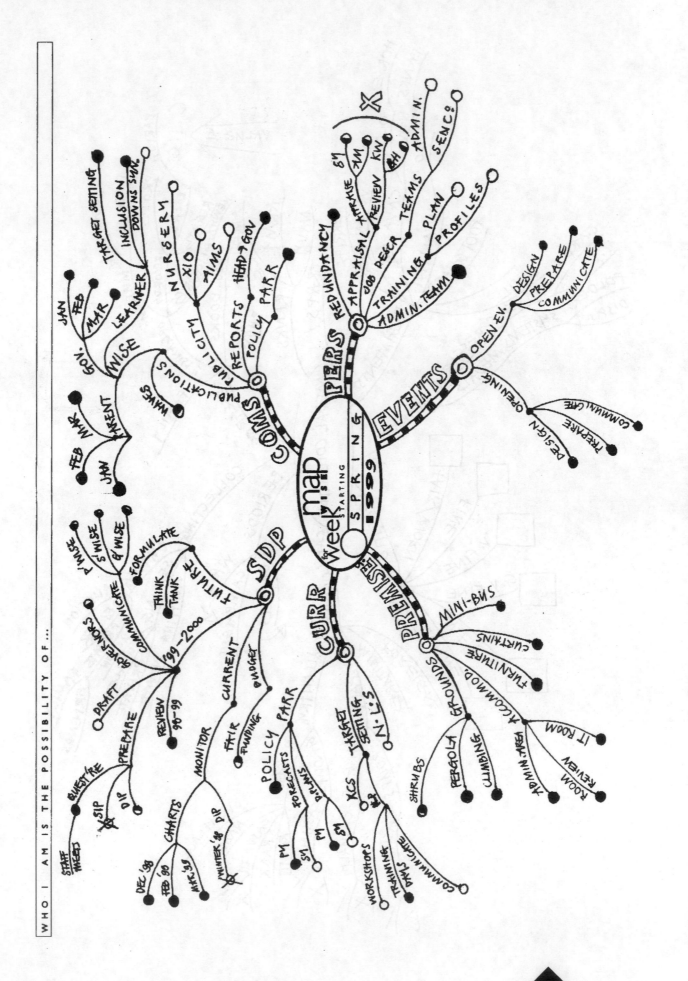

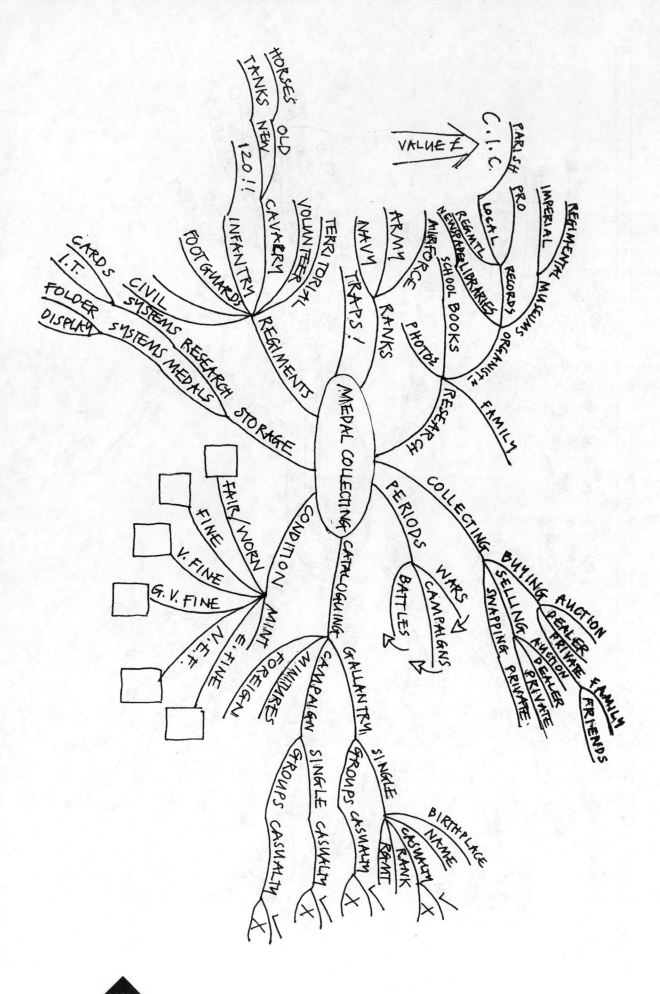

MAPWISE — accelerated learning through visible thinking

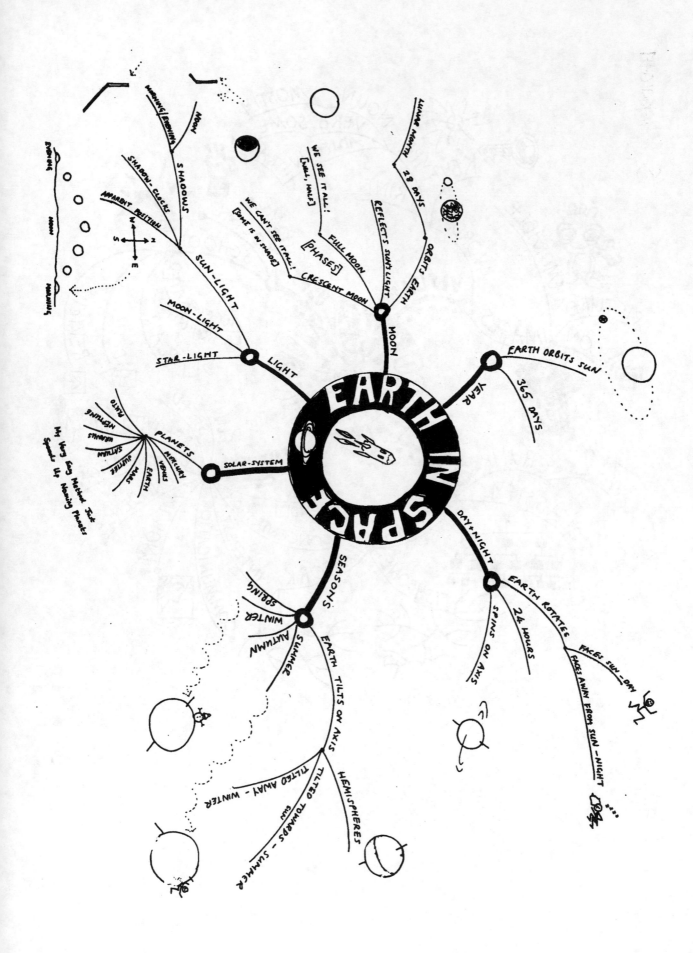

MAPWISE — accelerated learning through visible thinking

SARAH KNIGHT

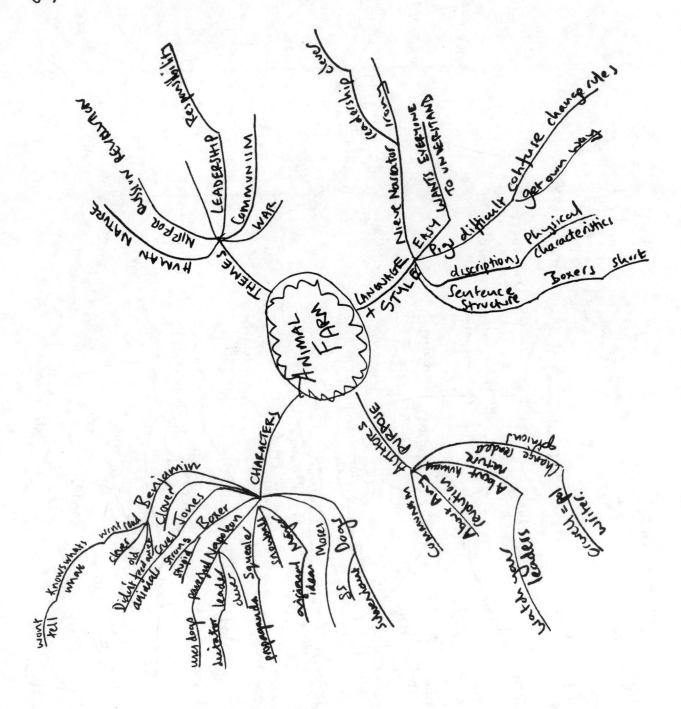

Animal Farm

THEMES
- LEADERSHIP
  - Stalin/Hitler
  - Communism
  - WAR
- HUMAN NATURE
  - Napoleon
  - Nazi/Russian Revolution

LANGUAGE + STYLE
- New Narrator (own)
  - (leadership) clones
  - dispassionate
- Easy Pig wants everyone to understand
  - difficult language change rules
  - get own way
- descriptions physical characteristics
  - Sentence structure
  - Boxers short

CHARACTERS
- Benjamin
  - wont read
  - knows whats
  - more
- Clover
  - old
  - Disillusioned animal
- Cruel Jones
- Boxer
  - strong
  - powerful
- Napoleon
  - dictator leader
  - cruel
- Squealer
  - propaganda
- Snowball
  - most original ideas
- Moses
- Dog
  - SS
  - food movements
- want kill

AUTHORS PURPOSE
- Communism revolution
- About human nature
- Orwell = writer (Russia readers physical)
- leaders victory

MAPWISE — accelerated learning through visible thinking

195

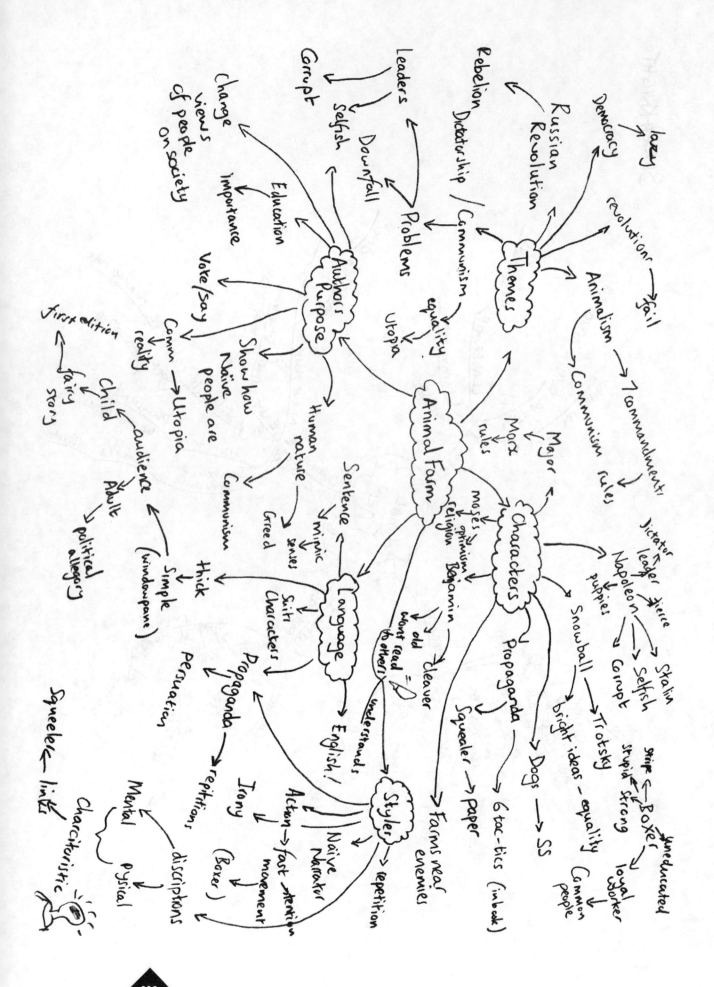

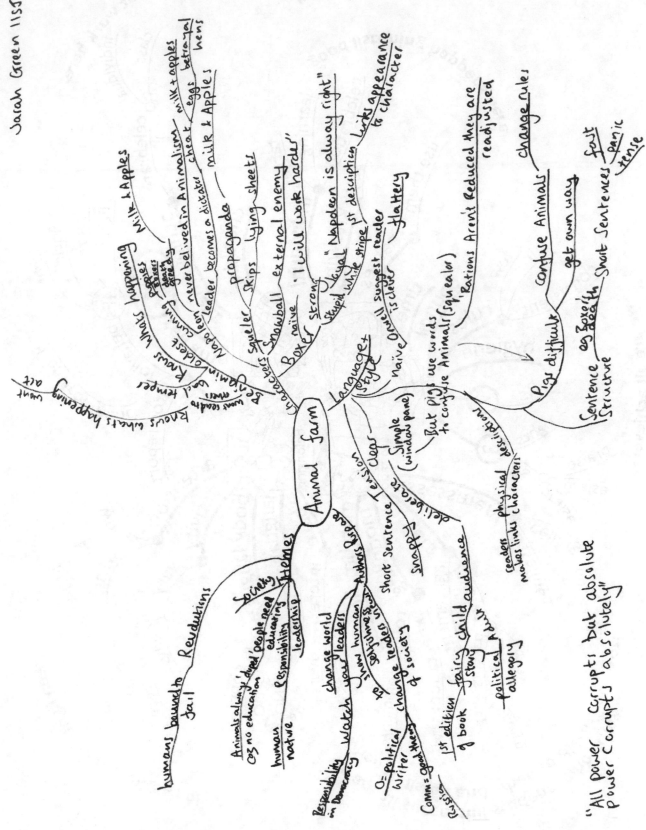

Sarah Green 11S5

Animal farm (central)

Characters:
- Milk & Apples
- never believed in Animalism — cheat milk + apples
- leader becomes a dictator — eggs, betrayal, hens
- Napoleon — cunning
- Propaganda
- Squealer — Skips, lying, sheets
- Snowball — external enemy
- Boxer — naïve, strong "I will work harder"
- "Napoleon is always right"
- stupid, loyal, white stripe — 1st description Links appearance to character
- Benjamin — knows oldest, bad temper, Knows what's happening but won't say anything
- Apples, poppies, pears, beer greedy
- Knows what's happening
- Horses what's happening
- Won't react to others
- flattery
- naïve Orwell is clever

Language + style:
- Simple (window pane)
- But pigs use words to confuse Animals (squealer)
- "Rations Aren't Reduced they are readjusted"
- readers Physical descriptions makes links characters
- Pigs difficult — confuse Animals get own way
- Sentence as Boxer's death — Short Sentences, fast, panic, tense
- Sentence Structure
- change rules
- Tension
- deliberate
- short sentence, snappy

Themes:
- Society
- Revolutions — humans bound to fail
- Animals always dupe cos no education, people need educating
- Responsibility — Leadership, human nature
- Authors Response — change world, watch your leaders
- new human society
- to confuse readers
- Responsibility in Democracy
- O = political writer
- Comm = Good sheets
- change readers of society
- Racism
- 1st edition fairy story, child audience
- book
- political allegory
- Adult audience

"All power Corrupts But absolute
Power Corrupts absolutely"

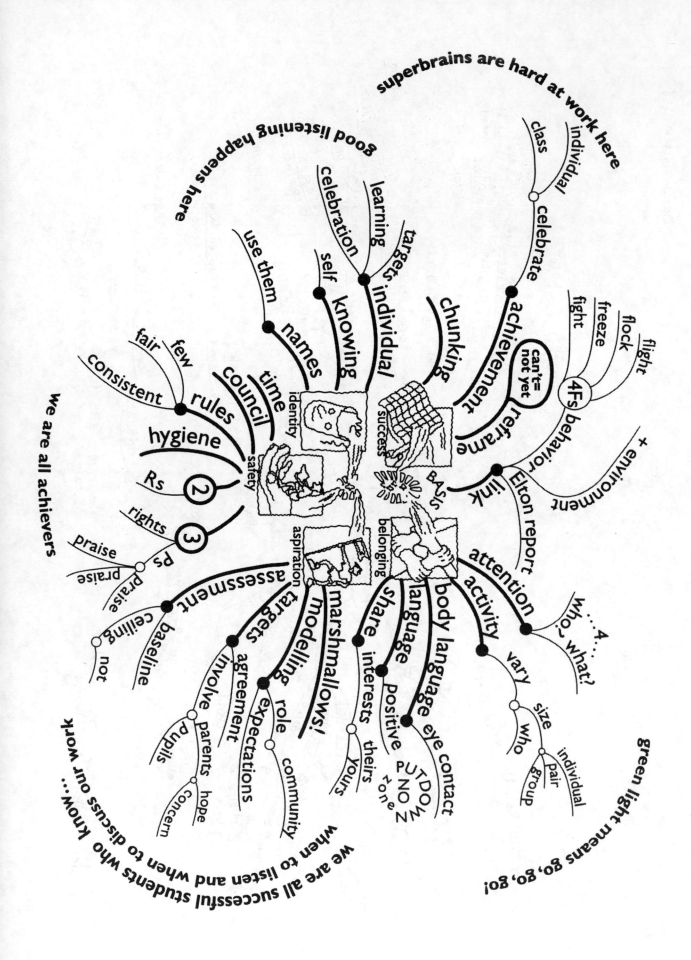

superbrains are hard at work here

Good listening happens here

We are all achievers

green light means go, go, go!

we are all successful students who know... when to listen and when to discuss our work

individual
class
celebrate
fight
freeze
flock
flight

4Fs behavior
can't = not yet
reframe
chunking
achievement

+ environment

Elton report
link
BASIS
attention
activity
vary
who
size
individual
pair
group
4..., who?, what?

learning
celebration
self
knowing
targets
individual
names
use them
time
council
rules
few
fair
consistent
hygiene
Rs
②
rights
③
Ps
praise
praise
praise
not
ceiling
baseline
assessment
targets
modelling
marshmallows!
belonging
share
language
body language
eye contact
positive
PUTDOWN ZONE
interests
theirs
yours
role
expectations
agreement
involve
parents
pupils
hope
concern
community

identity
success
safety
aspiration

MAPWISE — accelerated learning through visible thinking

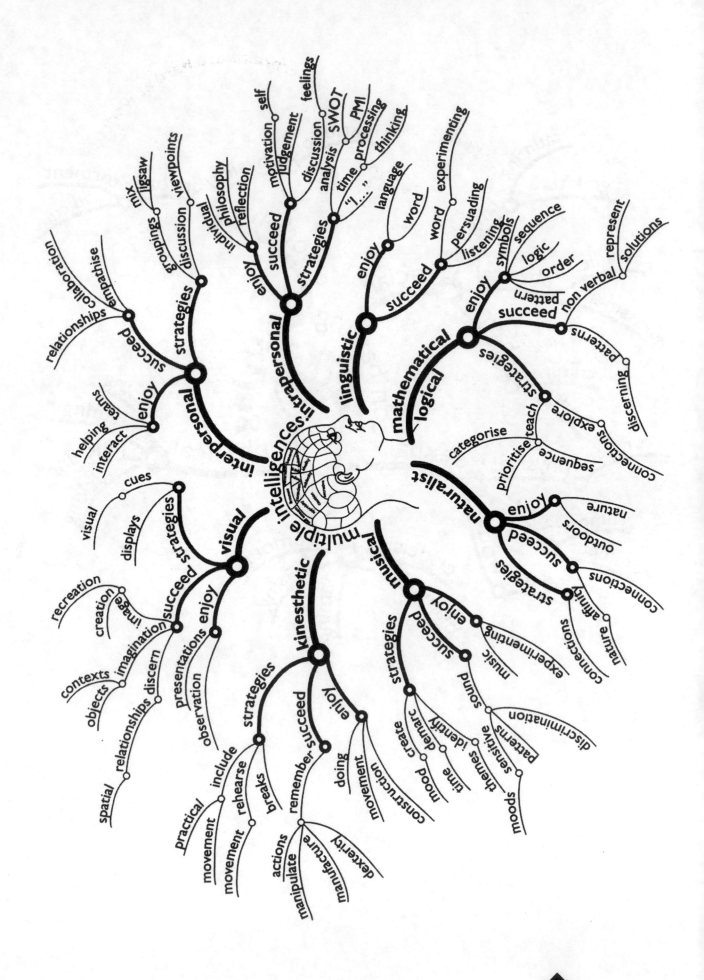

multiple intelligences

intrapersonal
- enjoy
  - individual
    - philosophy
    - reflection
  - discussion
    - viewpoints
- succeed
  - self
  - motivation
  - judgement
- strategies
  - discussion
  - analysis
    - SWOT
    - PMI
    - "I..."
    - time processing
    - thinking

interpersonal
- strategies
  - groupings
    - mix
    - jigsaw
- succeed
  - empathise
  - collaboration
  - relationships
- enjoy
  - teams
  - helping
  - interact

linguistic
- enjoy
  - language
  - word
- succeed
  - word
  - persuading
  - listening
- strategies

mathematical logical
- enjoy
  - symbols
  - sequence
  - logic
  - order
  - non verbal
    - represent
    - solutions
  - pattern
- succeed
  - patterns
  - discerning
- strategies
  - connections explore
  - teach
  - sequence
  - prioritise
  - categorise

naturalist
- enjoy
  - nature
  - outdoors
  - connections
  - nature affinity
- succeed
  - connections
  - experimenting
  - music
- strategies

musical
- enjoy
  - experimenting
  - music
  - sound
  - patterns
  - discrimination
- succeed
  - identify
  - demarc
  - create
  - construction
  - movement
  - doing
  - themes
  - time
  - mood
  - sensitive
  - moods
- strategies

kinesthetic
- enjoy
  - doing
  - movement
  - construction
- succeed
  - remember
    - manipulate
    - actions
    - dexterity
    - manufacture
  - rehearse
    - breaks
  - include
    - practical
    - movement
    - movement
- strategies
  - observation

visual
- enjoy
  - presentations
  - discern
  - imagination
    - image
    - creation
    - recreation
  - contexts
  - objects
  - relationships
  - spatial
- succeed
  - displays
  - visual
  - cues
- strategies

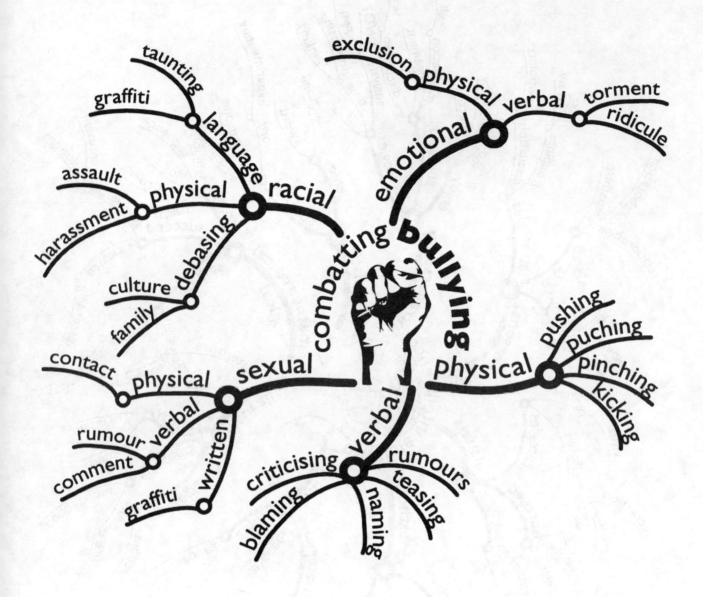

combatting **bullying**

emotional
- physical
  - exclusion
- verbal
  - torment
  - ridicule

physical
- pushing
- puching
- pinching
- kicking

verbal
- criticising
- blaming
- naming
- rumours
- teasing

racial
- language
  - taunting
  - graffiti
- physical
  - assault
  - harassment
- debasing
  - culture
  - family

sexual
- physical
  - contact
- verbal
  - rumour
  - comment
- written
  - graffiti

MAPWISE — accelerated learning through visible thinking

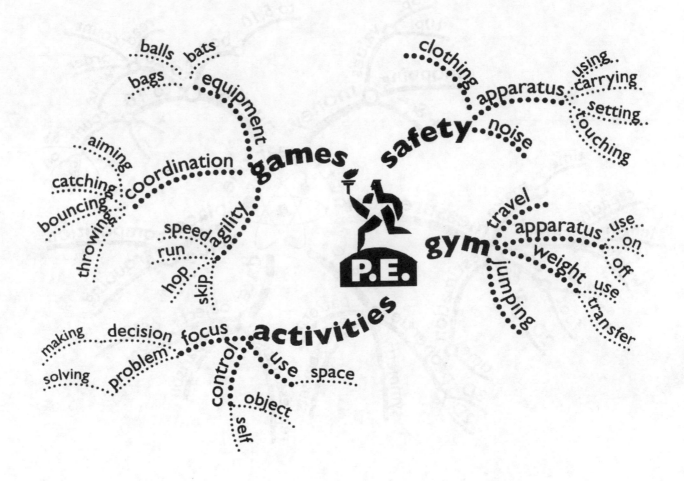

P.E.

games
- equipment
  - balls
  - bats
  - bags
- coordination
  - aiming
  - catching
  - bouncing
  - throwing
- agility
  - speed
  - run
  - hop
  - skip

safety
- clothing
- apparatus
  - using
  - carrying
  - setting
  - touching
- noise

gym
- travel
- apparatus
  - use
  - on
  - off
  - transfer
- weight use
- jumping

activities
- focus
  - decision
    - making
  - problem
    - solving
- control
  - use space
  - object
  - self

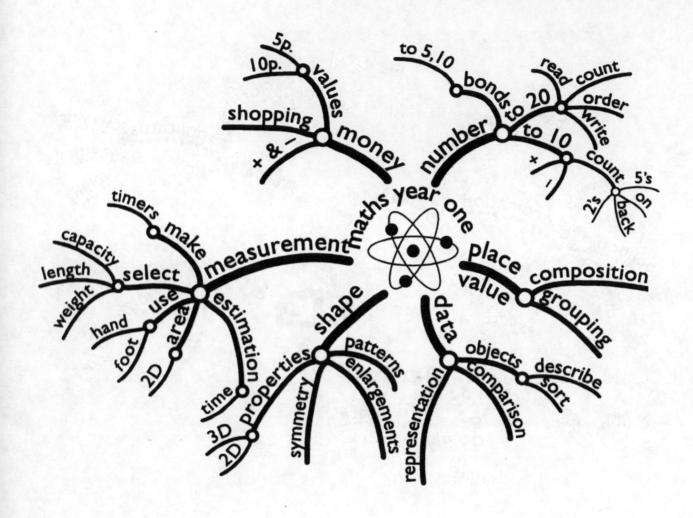

maths year one

number
- bonds
  - to 5,10
  - to 20
    - read
    - count
    - order
    - write
    - count
      - 5's
      - 2's
      - on
      - back
  - to 10
    - +
    - −

money
- values
  - 5p.
  - 10p.
- shopping
  - + & −

place value
- composition
- grouping

data
- objects
  - describe
  - sort
- comparison
- representation

shape
- patterns
- enlargements
- symmetry
- properties
  - 3D
  - 2D

measurement
- make
  - timers
- select
  - capacity
  - length
  - weight
  - hand
  - foot
- use
  - 2D
  - area
- estimation
  - time

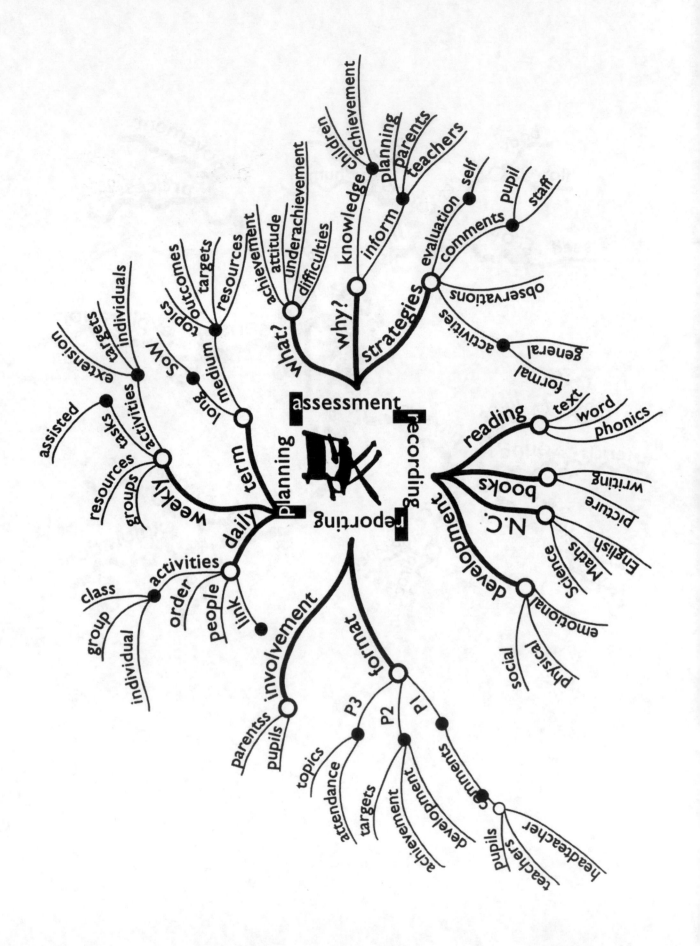

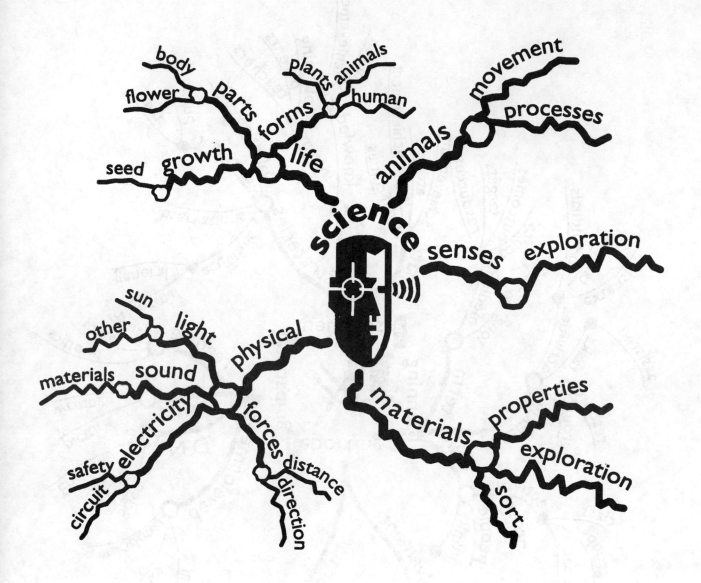

science

- parts
  - body
  - flower
- forms
  - plants
  - animals
  - human
- growth
  - seed
- life
- animals
  - movement
  - processes
- senses
  - exploration
- light
  - sun
  - other
- sound
  - materials
- physical
- electricity
  - safety
  - circuit
- forces
  - distance
  - direction
- materials
  - properties
  - exploration
  - sort

MAPWISE — accelerated learning through visible thinking

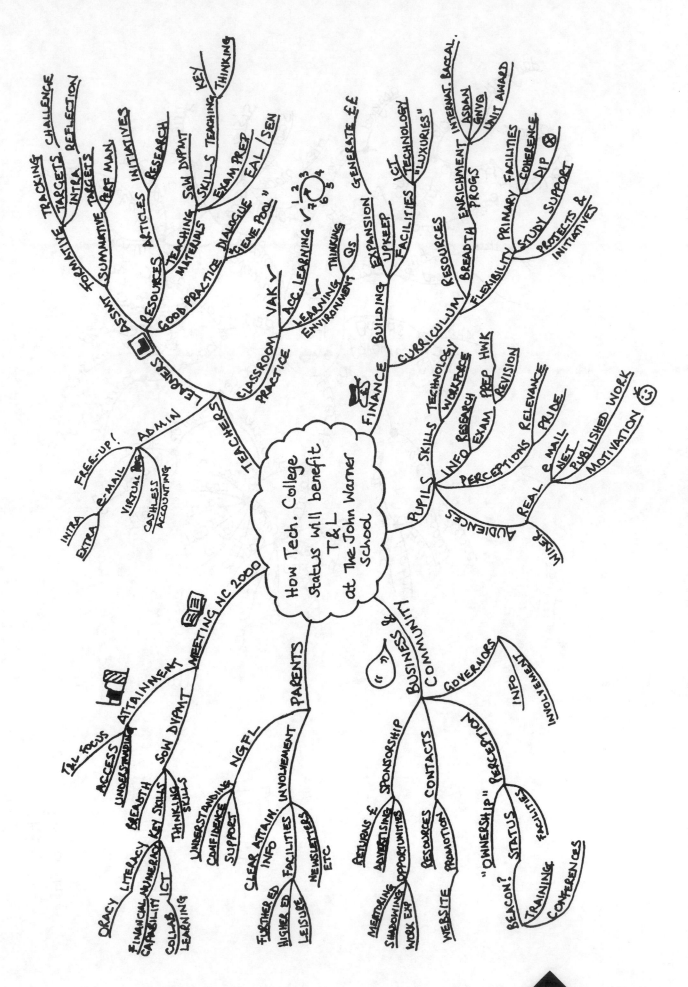

MAPWISE — accelerated learning through visible thinking

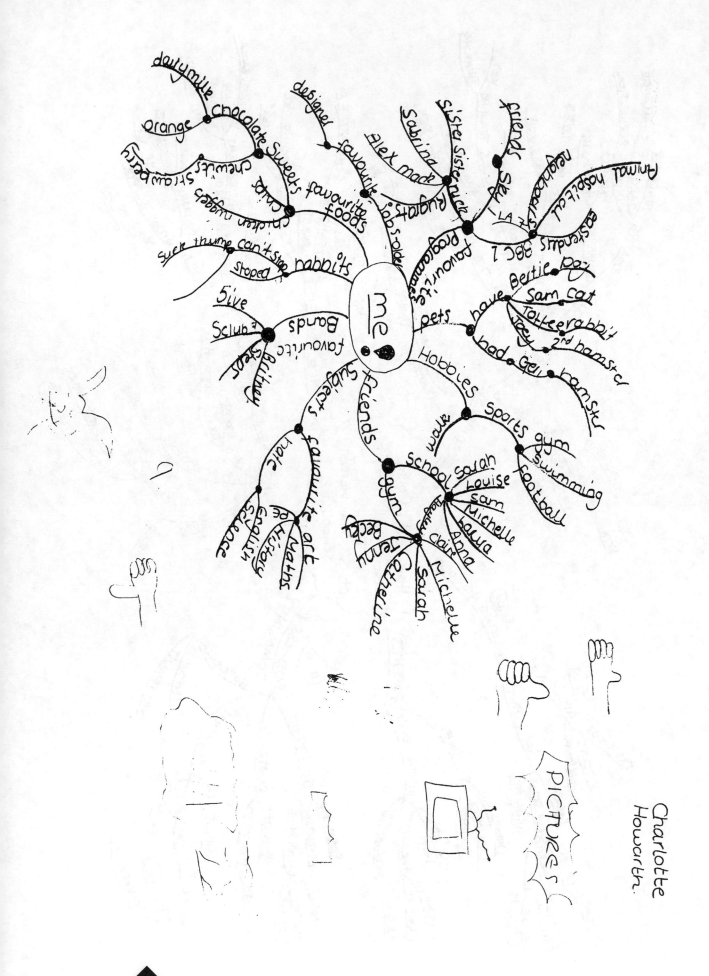

Charlotte
Howarth.

MAPWISE — accelerated learning through visible thinking

Laura Wenborn

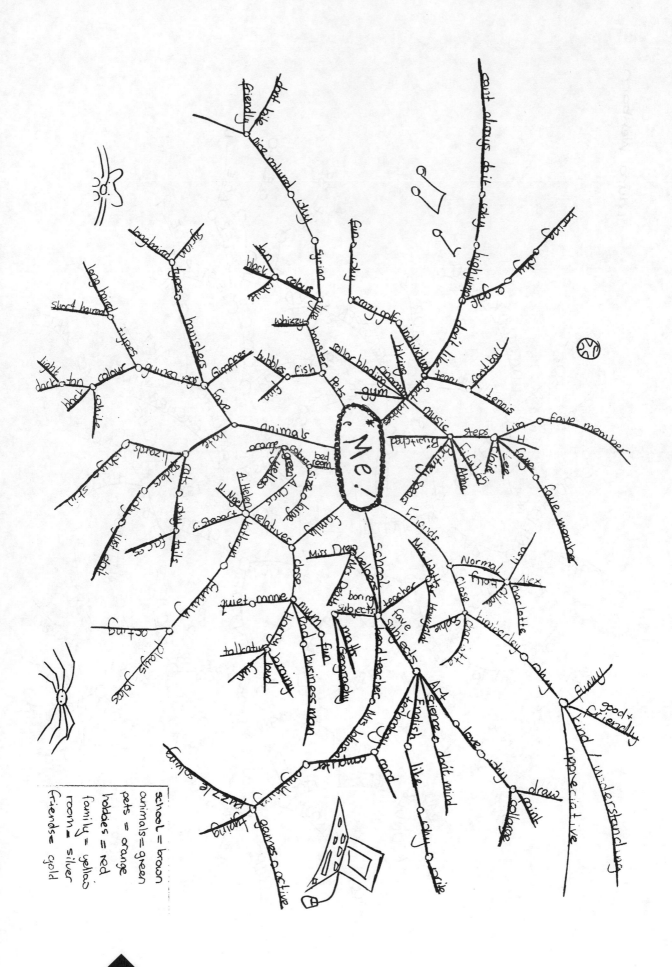

MAPWISE — accelerated learning through visible thinking

References & Acknowledgements

Every effort has been made to contact copyright holders of materials reproduced in this book. The publishers apologise for any omissions and will be pleased to rectify them at the earliest opportunity.

Introduction – The inside story

1   Blunkett, D. speaking prior to addressing the North of England Education Conference 5 January 2000, quoted in *Daily Express* 6 January 2000

2   McGuiness, C. (1999) 'From thinking skills to thinking schools', report for DfEE

3   Thornton, K. 'Teaching Wisdom That Stays Silent', *Times Educational Supplement*, 3 September 1999

4   'Excellence in Schools' (1997), report for DfEE

5   Beaver, D. (1994) *Lazy Learning*, Element, Dorset

6   Robbins, A. (1988) *Unlimited Power*, Simon and Schuster, London

7   Smith, A. and Call, N. (1999) *Accelerated Learning in Primary Schools*, Network Educational Press, Stafford

8   Kilpatrick, P., McCall, P. and Palmer, S. (1982), *I See What You Mean 2*, Oliver and Boyd, Edinburgh

Chapter 1 – Maps

1   Wurman, R. S. (1991) *Information Anxiety*, Pan, London

2   Rose, C. and Nicholl, M. J. (1997) *Accelerated Learning for the 21st Century*, Dell, New York

3   Goleman, D. (1990) *Meditative Mind*, Thorsons, London

4   Keates, J. S. (1982) *Understanding Maps*, Longman, Harlow

5   Avgerinou, M. and Ericson, J. (1997) 'A Review of the Concept of Visual Literacy', *British Journal of Educational Technology* Vol 28, No 4, Oct 1997 pp 280–291

6   Hodes, C. L. (1993) 'The Effect of Visual Mental Imagery on Speed and Accuracy of Information', in Braden, R. A., Baca, J. C. and Beauchamp D. G. (eds) *Art Science and Visual Literacy*, IVLA Blackburg, VA, pp 252–259

7   Smith, A. and Call, N., (1999) *Accelerated Learning in Primary Schools*, Network Educational Press, Stafford

8   Alder, H. and Heather, B. (1998) *NLP in 21 days*, Piatkus, London

9   Haber, R. N. (1970) 'How We Remember What We See', *Scientific American*, 105, May 1970

10   Lewin, J. R., Schriberg, L. K. and Berry J. K. (1983) 'A Concrete Strategy for Remembering Abstract Prose', American Educational Research Journal, Vol 20, pp 277–290 [copyright (1983) by the American Educational Research Association reproduced with permission from the publishers]

11   Long S. A., Winograd, P. N. and Bridge, C. A. (1989) 'The Effects of Reader and Text Characterstics and Imagery Repeated During and After Reading', *Reading Research Quarterly*, Vol 24, No 3, pp 313–372

12   Detheridge, T. and Detheridge, M. (1997) *Literacy Through Symbols*, David Fulton, London

13   Margulies, N. (1995) *Map It!*, Zephyr Press, Tucson

14   Wycoff, J. (1986) *Mindmapping*, Berkley Books, New York

15   Nickerson, R. S. in Buzan, T. (1993) *The Mindmap Book*, BBC, London, p 72

16   Buzan, T. (1974) *Use Your Head*, BBC, London

17   Seaborne, P. L. (1973) *Systems of Sets*, ESA Creative Learning, Harlow

18   Buzan, T. (1993) *The Mindmap Book*, BBC, London

19   Britton, J. (1970) *Language and Learning*, Pelican, London [reproduced by permission of Penguin Books Ltd.]

20   Novak, J. D. (1998) Learning, *Creating and Using Knowledge*, Lawrence Erlbaum, New Jersey, USA

21   McAleese, R. *A Theoretical View of Concept Mapping*, web page article on the difference between Concept Maps and Mind Maps™: www.icbl.hw.ac.uk/~granum/class/altdocs/vav._alt.htm

22   Heinich, R., Molenda, M., Russell, J. D. and Smaldino, S. E., (1996) *Instructional Media and Technologies for Learning – 5th edition*, Prentice–Hall, Englewood Cliffs, New Jersey

23   Carter, R. (1999) *Mapping the Mind*, Cassell & Co, London

24   Cohen, G. (1982) 'Theoretical Interpretations of Lateral Asymmetries' in Beaumont, J. (ed) *Divided Visual Field Studies of Cerebral Organisation*, Academic Press, London, pp 87–111

25   Riding, R. and Rayner, S. (1998) *Cognitive Styles and Learning Styles*, David Fulton, London

26   Smothermon, R. (1980) *Winning Through Enlightenment*, Context, San Francisco

27   Wenger, W. (1980) *The Einstein Factor*, Prima, California USA

28   Bannister, P. (1985) *Issues and Approaches in Personal Construct Theory*, Academic Press, London

29   Sternberg, R. J. (1997) *Thinking Styles*, Cambridge University Press, Cambridge

30   Novak, J. D. (1998) *Learning, Creating and Using Knowledge, Lawrence* Erlbaum, New York USA

31   Novak, J. D. and Gowin, D. B. (1984) *Learning How to Learn*, Cambridge University Press, Cambridge

32   Bower, G. H., Clark, M. C., Lesgold, A. M. and Winzenz, D. (1969) 'Hierarchical Retrieval Schemes in Recall of Categorised Word Lists', in *Journal of Verbal Learning Language and Verbal Behaviour*, 8, pp 323–43

33   Wenger, W. (1987) *How to Increase Your Intelligence*, D.O.K., East Aurora, New York USA

Chapter 2 – How to map

1   Britton, J. (1970) *Language and Learning*, Pelican, London [reproduced by permission of Penguin Books Ltd.]

2   Smith, A. and Call, N. (1999) *Accelerated Learning in Primary Schools*, Network Educational Press, Stafford

3   Novak, J. D. (1998) *Learning, Creating and Using Knowledge,* Lawrence Erlbaum Association, London

4   Alder, H. and Heather, B. (1998) *NLP in 21 days*, Piatkus, London

5   Svantesson, I. (1998) *Learning Maps and Memory Skills*, Kogan Page, London

6   Lake, M. (1999) private correspondance

7   De Bono, E. (1995) *Mind Power*, Dorling Kindersley, London

8   Wurman, R. S. (1991) *Information Anxiety*, Pan, London

Chapter 3 – Teaching mapping

1   McGuiness, C. (1999) 'From thinking skills to thinking schools', report for DfEE

2   Dryden, G. and Vos, J. (1994) *The Learning Revolution*, Accelerated Learning Systems Ltd, Aylesbury

3   Bruner, J. S. (1971) *Towards a theory of instruction*, Oxford University Press, Oxford

4   Novak, J. D. and Gowin, D. B. (1984) *Learning How to Learn*, Cambridge University Press, Cambridge

5   Woditsch, G. A. (1991) *The Thoughtful Teacher's Guide to Thinking Skills*, Lawrence Erlbaum, New Jersey, USA

6   Novak, J. D. (1998) *Learning, Creating and Using Knowledge,* Lawrence Erlbaum Association, London

7   Davis, W. S. and McCormack, A. (1979) *The Information Age*, Addison-Wesley, Reading MA

8   De Bono, E. (1995) *Mind Power*, Dorling Kindersley, London

9   Wurman, R. S. (1991) *Information Anxiety*, Pan, London

Chapter 4 — Thinking skills

1   Blunkett, D. Minister for Education, speaking before addressing North of England Education Conference, 5 January 2000, quoted in *Daily Express* 6 January 2000

2   McGuiness, C. (1999) 'From thinking skills to thinking schools', report for DfEE

3   De Bono, E. (1976) *Teaching Thinking*, Temple Smith, London

4   Feuerstein, R., Rand, Y., Hoffman, M. and Miller, R. (1980) *Instrumental Enrichment*, University Park Press, Baltimore USA

5   Blagg, N. (1991) *Can We Teach Intelligence?*, Lawrence Erlbaum, New York

6   De Bono, E. (1981) CoRT, Pergamon, Oxford

7   Lipman, M., Sharp, A. N., Oscanyon, F. S. (1980) *Philosophy in the Classroom*, Temple University Press, Philadelphia USA

8   Blagg, N. (1988), *Somerset Thinking Skills*, Blackwell, Oxford

9   Lake. M. and Needham, M. (1990) *Top Ten Thinking Tactics*, Questions Publishing, Birmingham

10   Lake, M. (1989) *Brill the Brave*, Questions Publishing, Birmingham

11   Lake, M. (1996) *Brill and the Riddle of the Whirlwind*, Questions Publishing, Birmingham

12   Fisher, R. (1996) *Stories for Thinking*, Nash Pollock, Oxford

13   Fisher, R. (1999) *Stories for Thinking*, Nash Pollock, Oxford

14   Murris, K. (1989) *Philosophy Through Picture Books*, Infonet Publications, London

15   Fisher, R. (1996) *Stories for Thinking*, Nash Pollock, Oxford

16   Fisher, R. (1999) *Poems for Thinking*, Nash Pollock, Oxford

17   Fisher, R. (1997) *Games for Thinking*, Nash Pollock, Oxford

18   Fisher, R. (2000) *Pictures for Thinking*, Nash Pollock, Oxford

19   *Sharp Eye* (2000), Ginn & Co, London

20   *Cognitive Acceleration in Science Education* (CASE)

21   Ausubel, D. P. (1978) *Educational Psychology: A cognitive View*, Second Edition, Holt/Reinhart, New York USA

22   McPeck, J. E. (1990) *Teaching Critical Thinking*, Routledge, London

23   Sternberg, R. (1973) 'Intelligence and non-entrenchment', *Journal of Educational Psychology* Vol 73, No 1, Feb 1981, pp 1–16

24   Ryle, G. (1949) *The Concept of Mind*, Barnes and Noble, New York USA

25   Ornstein, R. and Ehrlich, P. (1991), *New World, New Mind*, Paladin, London

26   Britton, J. (1970) *Language and Learning*, Pelican, London [reproduced by permission of Penguin Books Ltd.]

27   Postman, N. (1990) *Teaching as a Conserving Activity*, Delacorte, New York, USA

28   Bruner, J. (1960) *Process of Education*, Vintage Books, New York USA

29   Schwab, J. J. (1970) 'Structures of the disciplines: Meanings and Slogans', in Snook, I. A. (1970) 'The Concept of Indoctrination', *Studies in Philosophy and Education*, Vol 7, No 2, Fall 1970

30   Wurman, R. S. (1991) *Information Anxiety*, Pan, London

31   Lake, M. (1995) personal correspondence

32   McGuiness, C. (1999) 'From thinking skills to thinking schools', report for DfEE

Chapter 5 — Teaching and learning systems

1   O'Connor, J. and McDermott, I. (1997) *The Art of Systems Thinking*, Thorsons, California USA

2   Fisher, R. (1995) *Teaching Children to Learn*, Stanley Thornes, Cheltenham [reproduced with the permission of Stanley Thornes Publishers Ltd.]

3   Hughes, M. (1999) *Closing the Learning Gap*, Network Educational Press, Stafford

4   Novak, J. D. and Gowin, D. B. (1984) *Learning How to Learn*, Cambridge University Press, Cambridge

5   Jensen, E. (1995) *Super Teaching*, The Brain Store Inc, USA

6   Wurman, R. S. (1991) *Information Anxiety*, Pan, London

7   Woditsch, G. A. (1991) *The Thoughtful Teacher's Guide to Thinking Skills*, Lawrence Erlbaum, New Jersey, USA

8   Buzan, T. (1993) *The Mindmap Book*, BBC, London

9   Kerry, T. (1998) *Questioning and Explaining in Classrooms*, Hodder and Stoughton, London

10   Novak, J. D. (1998) *Learning, Creating and Using Knowledge*, Lawrence Erlbaum Association, London

11   Perkins, D. N. (1987) 'Thinking Frames: An Integrating Perspective on Teaching Cognitive Skills', in Baron, J. and Sternberg, R. (1987) *Teaching Thinking Skills: Theory and Research*, W H Freeman, New York

12   Katz, L. G. (September 1993) 'Dispositions as Educational Goals', *ERIC DIGEST*, University of Illinois

13   Henderson, P. (1993) *How to Succeed in Examinations and Assessments – National Extension College*, Collins Educational, London

Chapter 6 — Maps in the classroom

1   Fisher, R. (1995) *Teaching Children to Learn*, Stanley Thornes, Cheltenham [reproduced with the permission of Stanley Thornes Publishers Ltd.]

2   Wragg, E. C. and Brown, G. (1993) *Explaining*, Routledge, London

3   Novak, J. D. (1998) *Learning, Creating and Using Knowledge*, Lawrence Erlbaum Association, London

4   Smith, A. and Call, N. (1999) *Accelerated Learning in the Primary School*, Network Educational Press, Stafford

5   Smith, A. (1998) *Accelerated Learning in Practice*, Network Educational Press, Stafford

6   Jensen, E. (1995) *Super Teaching*, The Brain Store Inc, USA

7   Smith, A. (1996) *Accelerated Learning in the Classroom*, Network Educational Press, Stafford

8   Hughes, M. (1999) *Closing the Learning Gap*, Network Educational Press, Stafford

9   Wenger, W. and Poe, R. (1990) *The Einstein Factor*, Prima Publishing, Rocklin, California

10   Ostrander, S. and Schroeder, L. (1994) *Superlearning 2000*, Souvenir Press, London

11   Novak, J. D. and Gowin, D. B. (1984) *Learning How to Learn*, Cambridge University Press, Cambridge

12   Baddeley, A. D. (1995) 'Memory', in French, C. C. and Colman A. M. (eds) *Cognitive Psychology*, Longman, London

Chapter 7 — Cleverness and internal maps

1   Greenfield, S. (November 1999) 'The State of the Art of the Science of Brain Research'; paper presented at the Royal Institution, London

2   McGuiness, C. (1999) 'From thinking skills to thinking schools', report for DfEE

3   Wurman, R. S. (1991) *Information Anxiety*, Pan, London

4   Bruer, J. T. (1997) 'Education and the Brain: A Bridge Too Far', *Educational Researcher*, Vol 26, No 8, Nov 1997 [copyright (1997) by the American Educational Research Association reproduced with permission from the publishers]

5   Senge, P. (1994) *Fifth Discipline Fieldbook*, Nicholas Brearley, London

6   Goleman, D. (1985) *Vital Lies, Simple Truths*, Bloomsbury, London

7   Kelly, G. A. (1963) *A Theory of Personality*, Norton, New York [copyright © 1955, 1963 by George A. Kelly, renewed 1983, 1991 by Gladys Kelly, reprinted by permission of WW Norton & Co]

8   Rumelhart, D. E. (1980) 'Schemata: The Building Bricks of Cognition', in Spiro, R. J., Bruce, B. C. and Brewer, W. F. (eds), *Theoretical Issues in Reading Comprehension*, Lawrence Erlbaum, New York USA

9   Sherwood, D. (1988) *Unlock Your Mind*, Gower, Aldershot

10   Marshall, S. P. (1995) *Schemas in Problem Solving*, Cambridge University Press, Cambridge

11   Quin, P. (1987) 'The Categorical Representations of Visual Pattern Information by Young Infants', *Cognition* 27, 145–179

12   Johnson, M. (1987) *The Body in the Mind: the Bodily Basis of Meaning, Imagination and Reason*, University of Chicago Press, London

13   Britton, J. (1970) *Language and Learning*, Pelican, London [reproduced by permission of Penguin Books Ltd.]

14   Woditsch, G. A. (1991) *The Thoughtful Teacher's Guide to Thinking Skills*, Lawrence Erlbaum, New Jersey, USA.

15   Novak, J. D. (1998) *Learning, Creating and Using Knowledge*, Lawrence Erlbaum, New Jersey

16   Schon, D. (1991) *The Reflective Practioner*, Arena, Aldershot

17   Schooler, J. (1998) in Claxton, G. *Hare Brain, Tortoise Mind*, Fourth Estate, London [reprinted by permission of Fourth Estate Ltd., copyright © (1997) Guy Claxton]

18   Miller, P. (1998) *Mobilising the Power of What You Know*, Random House, London

19   Van Nagel, C., Reese, E. J., Reese, M. and Siudzinski, R. (1985) *Mega Teaching and Learning*, Metamorphous Press, Portland, Oregon USA

20   Fisher, R. (1995) *Teaching Children to Learn*, Stanley Thornes, Cheltenham [reproduced with the permission of Stanley Thornes Publishers Ltd.]

Other titles from Network Educational Press

ACCELERATED LEARNING SERIES

General Editor: **Alistair Smith**
MapWise is the third book in the Accelerated Learning Series. The other books in the series are detailed below.

Book 1: *Accelerated Learning in the Practice* by Alistair Smith
- The author's second book that takes Nobel Prize winning brain research into the classroom.
- Structured to help readers access and retain the information necessary to begin to accelerate their own learning and that of the students they teach.
- Includes 9 principles of learning based on brain research and the author's 7-stage Accelerated Learning cycle.

Book 2: *the alps approach: accelerated learning in primary schools* by Alistair Smith and Nicola Call
- Shows how research on how we learn, collected by Alistair Smith, can be used to great effect in the primary classroom.
- Provides practical and accessible examples of strategies used by highly experienced primary teach Nicola Call, at a school where the SATs results shot up as a consequence.
- Professional, practical and exhilarating resource that gives readers the opportunity to develop the ALPS approach for themselves and for the children in their care.

Book 4: *the alps resource book* by Alistair Smith and Nicola Call
A follow-up to the best-selling alps approach, it provides photocopiable resource for teachers to use in the classroom.
- Affirmation posters for the classroom
- The 100 best homeworks
- How to make target setting easy, fun and useful
- 101 Brain Break activities that connect to learning

Bright Sparks: Motivational posters for pupils by Alistair Smith
Over 100 photocopiable posters to help motivate pupils and help improve their learning.
- The magic spelling strategy
- How you learn best
- The abc of motivation
- Exam technique

Leading Learning: Staff development posters for schools by Alistair Smith
With over 200 posters which draw from the best in brain research from around the world.
- 5 features of learning to learn
- Smart marking
- Target setting
- Thinking skills

THE SCHOOL EFFECTIVENESS SERIES

Book 1: *Accelerated Learning in the Classroom* by Alistair Smith
- The first book in the UK to apply new knowledge about the brain to classroom practice
- Aims to increase the pace of learning and deepen understanding
- Offers practical solutions on improving performance, motivation and understanding

Book 2: *Effective Learning Activities* by Chris Dickinson
- An essential teaching guide which focuses on practical activities to improve learning
- Includes activities which are designed to promote differentiation and understanding
- Offers advice on how to maximise the use of available – and limited – resources
- Includes activities suitable for GCSE, National Curriculum, Highers, GSVQ and GNVQ

Book 3: *Effective Heads of Department* by Phil Jones & Nick Sparks
- ◆ An ideal support for Heads of Department looking to develop necessary management skills
- Designed to develop practice in line with OFSTED expectations and DfEE thinking by monitoring and improving quality
- Addresses issues such as managing resources, leadership, learning, departmental planning and making assessment valuable

Book 4: *Lessons are for Learning* by Mike Hughes
- Encourages teachers to reflect on their own classroom practice and challenges them to think about why they teach in the way they do
- Develops a clear picture of what constitutes effective classroom practice
- Offers practical suggestions for activities that bridge the gap between recent developments in the theory of learning and the constraints of classroom teaching
- Ideal for stimulating thought and generating discussion

Book 5: *Effective Learning in Science* by Paul Denley and Keith Bishop
- Looks at planning for effective learning within the context of science
- Encourages discussion about the aims and purposes in teaching science and the role of subject knowledge in effective teaching
- Tackles issues such as planning for effective learning, the use of resources and other relevant management issues

Book 6: *Raising Boys' Achievement* by Jon Pickering
- Addresses the causes of boys' underachievement and offers possible solutions
- Focuses the search for causes and solutions on teachers working in the classrooms
- Looks at examples of good practice in schools to help guide the planning and implementation of strategies to raise achievement

Book 7: *Effective Provision for Able & Talented Children* by Barry Teare
- Basic theory, necessary procedures and turning theory into practice
- Main methods of identifying the able and talented
- Concerns about achievement and appropriate strategies to raise achievement
- The role of the classroom teacher, monitoring and evaluation techniques

Book 8: *Effective Careers Education & Guidance* by Andrew Edwards and Anthony Barnes
- Strategic planning of the careers programme as part of the wider curriculum
- Practical consideration of managing careers education and guidance
- Practical activities for reflection and personal learning, and case studies where such activities have been used

Book 9: *Best behaviour and Best behaviour FIRST AID* by Peter Relf, Rod Hirst, Jan Richardson and Georgina Youdell
- Provides support for those who seek starting points for effective behaviour management, for individual teachers and for middle and senior managers
- Focuses on practical and useful ideas for individual schools and teachers

Best behaviour FIRST AID (pack of 5 booklets)
- Provides strategies to cope with aggression, defiance and disturbance
- Straightforward action points for self-esteem

Book 10: *The Effective School Governor* by David Marriott
(including free audio tape)
- Straightforward guidance on how to fulfil a governor's role and responsibilities
- Develops your personal effectiveness as an individual governor
- Practical support on how to be an effective member of the governing team
- Audio tape for use in car or at home

Book 11: *Improving Personal Effectiveness for Managers in Schools* by James Johnson
- An invaluable resource for new and experienced teachers in both primary and secondary schools
- Contains practical strategies for improving leadership and management skills
- Focuses on self-management skills, managing difficult situations, working under pressure, developing confidence, creating a team ethos and communicating effectively

217

Book 12: *Making Pupil Data Powerful* by Maggie Pringle and Tony Cobb
- Shows teachers in primary, middle and secondary schools how to interpret pupils' performance data and how to use it to enhance teaching and learning
- Provides practical advice on analysing performance and learning behaviours, measuring progress, predicting future attainment, setting targets and ensuring continuity and progression

Book 13: *Closing the Learning Gap* by Mike Hughes
- Helps teachers, departments and schools to close the Learning Gap between what we know about effective learning and what actually goes on in the classroom
- Helps teachers to apply recent research findings about the brain and learning
- Full of practical advice and real, tested strategies for improvement

Book 14: *Getting Started* by Henry Leibling
- Provides invaluable advice for Newly Qualified Teachers (NQTs) during the three-term induction period that comprises their first year of teaching.
- Advice includes strategies on how to get to know the school and the new pupils, how to work with induction tutors, and when to ask for help.

Book 15: *Leading the Learning School* by Colin Weatherley
- Learning – 13 key principles of learning are derived from a survey of up-to-date knowledge of the brain and learning
- Teaching – how to use the key principles of learning to improve teachers' professional knowledge and skills, make the learning environment more supportive and improve the design of learning activities

Book 16: *Adventures in Learning* by Mike Tilling
- Integrate other theories about how we learn into a coherent 'vision' of learning that unfolds over time
- Recognise the phases of the Learner's Journey and make practical interventions at key moments
- Shape the experience of learners from the 'micro' level of the individual lesson to the 'macro' level of the learning lifetime

Book 17: *Strategies for Closing the Learning Gap* by Mike Hughes with Andy Vass
- Highlights and simplifies key issues emerging from the latest discoveries about how the human brain learns
- Offers proven, practical strategies and suggestions as to how to apply this new research in the classroom, to improve students' learning and help them achieve their full potential
- Written and arranged in the same easy-to-read style as *Closing the Learning Gap*, to encourage teachers to browse through it during 'spare' moments

Book 18: *Classroom Management* by Philip Waterhouse and Chris Dickinson
- Full of practical ideas to help teachers find ways of integrating Key Skills and Thinking Skills into an already overcrowded curriculum
- Shows how Induction Standards, OFSTED requirements and the findings of the Hay McBer report into School Effectiveness can be met or implemented through carefully thought out strategies for the management and organisation of the classroom

EDUCATION PERSONNEL MANAGEMENT SERIES

These new Education Personnel Management handbooks will help headteachers, senior managers and governors to manage a broad range of personnel issues.

The Well Teacher – management strategies for beating stress, promoting staff health and reducing absence
by Maureen Cooper
- Provides straightforward, practical advice on how to deal strategically with staff absenteeism, which can be so expensive in terms of sick pay and supply cover, through proactively promoting staff health.

- Includes suggestions for reducing stress levels in schools.
- Outlines ways in which to deal with individual cases of staff absence.

Managing Challenging People – dealing with staff conduct
by Bev Curtis and Maureen Cooper
- Deals with managing staff whose conduct gives cause for concern.
- Summarises the employment relationship in schools, as well as those areas of education and employment law relevant to staff discipline.
- Looks at the differences between conduct and capability, and between misconduct and gross misconduct.

Managing Poor Performance – handling staff capability issues
by Bev Curtis and Maureen Cooper
- Explains clearly why capability is important in providing an effective and high quality education for pupils.
- Outlines the legal position and the role of governors in dealing with the difficult issues surrounding poor performance.
- Details the various stages of formal capability procedures and dismissal hearings.

Managing Allegations Against Staff – personnel and child protection issues in schools
by Maureen Cooper
- Provides invaluable advice to headteachers, senior managers and personnel staff on how to deal with the difficult issues arising from accusations made against school employees.
- Shows what schools can do to protect students, while safeguarding employees from the potentially devastating consequences of false allegations.

Managing Recruitment and Selection – appointing the best staff
by Bev Curtis and Maureen Cooper
- Guides schools through the legal minefield of anti-discrimination, human rights and other legislation relevant when making appointments.
- Provides senior managers and staffing committees with help in many areas, including developing effective selection procedures, creating job descriptions and personnel specifications, writing better job advertisements and short-listing and interviewing techniques.

Managing Redundancies – dealing with reduction and reorganisation of staff
by Bev Curtis and Maureen Cooper
- Provides guidance in how to handle fairly and carefully the unsettling and sensitive issue of making staff redundant.
- Gives independent advice on keeping staff informed of their options, employment and other relevant legislation, sources of support (including the LEA) and working to the required time-scales.

VISIONS OF EDUCATION SERIES

The Unfinished Revolution by John Abbott and Terry Ryan
- Draws on evidence from the past to show how shifting attitudes in society and politics have shaped Western education systems.
- Argues that what is now needed is a completely fresh approach, designed around evidence about how children actually learn.

The Child is Father of the Man by John Abbott
Also from one of the authors of 'The Unfinished Revolution'. The book outlines how his ideas about schools, thinking, learning and teaching have developed.

The Learning Revolution by Jeanette Vos and Gordon Dryden
The book includes a huge wealth of data and research from around the world.
- The 16 main trends to shape tomorrow's world
- The 13 steps to create a learning society
- The 20 steps to teach yourself anything you need
- The 12 steps to transform an education system
- How to change the way the world learns

Wise-Up by Guy Claxton
> The book teaches us how to raise children who are curious and confident explorers, and how we ourselves can learn to pair problem-solving with creativity. This is essential and compelling reading for parents, educators and managers alike.

THE LITERACY COLLECTION

Helping With Reading by Anne Butterworth and Angela White
- Includes sections on 'Hearing Children Read', Word Recognition' and 'Phonics'.
- Provides precisely focused, easily implemented follow-up activities for pupils who need extra reinforcement of basic reading skills.
- Provides clear, practical and easily implemented activities that directly relate to the National Curriculum and 'Literacy Hour' group work. Ideas and activities can also be incorporated into Individual Education Plans.

Class Talk by Rosemary Sage
- Looks at how students talk in different classroom situations and evaluates this information in terms of planning children's learning.
- Considers the problems of transmitting meaning to others.
- Discusses and reflects on practical strategies to improve the quality of talking, teaching and learning.

OTHER TITLES FROM NEP

Effective Resources for Able and Talented Children by Barry Teare
- A practical sequel to Barry Teare's Effective Provision for Able and Talented Children (see above), which can nevertheless be used entirely independently.
- Contains a wealth of photocopiable resources for able and talented pupils in both the primary and secondary sectors.

More Effective Resources for Able and Talented Children by Barry Teare
- A treasury of stimulating and challenging activities to provide excitement and enrichment for more able children of all ages.
- can be used in situations both within and beyond normal classroom lessons, including differentiated homework, summer schools, clubs and competitions.
- Resources are divided into several themes: English and literacy; mathematics and numeracy; science; humanities, citizenship, problem solving, decision making and information processing; modern foreign languages; young children; logical thought; detective work and codes; lateral thinking; competitions.

Imagine That... by Stephen Bowkett
- Hands-on, user-friendly manual for stimulating creative thinking, talking and writing in the classroom.
- Empowers children to learn how to learn.

Self-Intelligence by Stephen Bowkett
- Helps explore and develop emotional resourcefulness in teachers and their pupils.
- Aims to help teachers and pupils develop the high-esteem that underpins success in education.

Index

Illustrations or maps that appear on a different page from the accompanying text have been indexed separately, and are indicated by page references in *bold italic*.